Contents

		Page
ACKNOWLEDGMENTS		v
PHOTO CREDITS		vi
PREFACE		vii
CHAPTER 1	The Editing Process	1
CHAPTER 2	News Editing Style	9
CHAPTER 3	Language Usage	33
CHAPTER 4	Writing Headlines	53
CHAPTER 5	Selecting News	69
CHAPTER 6	Handling Features and Special Stories	95
CHAPTER 7	Publicity Releases	143
CHAPTER 8	Handling Wire Copy	173
CHAPTER 9	Dangerous Copy	183
CHAPTER 10	Typography	209
CHAPTER 11	Graphics	223
CHAPTER 12	Photo Editing	229
CHAPTER 13	Makeup & Design	239
CHAPTER 14	Proofreading	273
CHAPTER 15	Broadcast Editing	281
APPENDIX A	Editing Symbols	293
APPENDIX B	Headline Schedule	295
APPENDIX C	State Map	297
APPENDIX D	City Directory	299

THE EDITORIAL PROCESS

2nd Edition

Dan L. Lattimore
Colorado State University

John W. Windhauser
Louisiana State University

Morton Publishing Company
295 W. Hampden, Suite 104
Englewood, Colorado 80110

Copyright © 1984 by Morton Publishing Company

All rights reserved. No part of this book may be reproduced in any form or by any electronic or mechanical means, including photocopying and recording, or by any information storage or retrieval system without permission in writing from the publisher.

ISBN: 0-89582-115-X

Printed in the United States of America

Acknowledgments

In preparation of the second edition of *The Editorial Process* we especially thank Jean Lundberg, Colorado State University, for preparation of chapters on typography and graphics and advice throughout the book. Elinor Grusin of Ohio University also provided an extensive review and comments for inclusion of material in this edition. Walter Stewart of the University of Northern Colorado, Louis Day of Louisiana State University, Liz Watts of Kearney State University, and George Winford of the University of Alaska deserve special recognition for their helpful advice and comments.

The photographs used in this text were provided by James Dean, editor of the Fort Collins Coloradoan; Steve Walters, managing editor of the Temple Daily Telegram; Ed Swartley, business editor of the Colorado Springs Sun; Ed Lehman, editor and publisher of the Longmont Times-Call; and Robert Spiegel, editor of the Wisconsin State Journal. We greatly appreciate their sharing the photographs for this edition.

Special thanks also should be given to Cheryl Henderson, Darlene Fowler, John Brooks, Mary Lindberg, Gigi Guyton, and Robert Greving for their assistance in preparation of the manuscript.

Photo Credits

Cover Photo	Ft. Collins Coloradoan
Chapter 1	Ft. Collins Coloradoan Wisconsin State Journal
Chapter 2	Longmont Times Call
Chapter 3	Longmont Times Call
Chapter 5	Temple Daily Telegram
Chapter 6	Ft. Collins Coloradoan
Chapter 7	Keystone
Chapter 8	Colorado State Journalist
Chapter 10	Ft. Collins Coloradoan Temple Daily Telegram
Chapter 11	Temple Daily Telegram Longmont Times Call
Chapter 12	Ft. Collins Coloradoan
Chapter 13	Temple Daily Telegram Ft. Collins Coloradoan
Chapter 14	Colorado Springs Sun
Chapter 15	Water Management Synthesis Project

Preface

The editorial process begins with creative news assignments and ends when the final page proof is read. In between are tasks for many people. The principal job that must be learned in the editorial process, though, is that of copy editor.

The copy editor edits copy and writes headlines. Through a number of copy editing and headline writing exercises we have attempted to provide ample practice in performing these basic copy editing functions in this worktext. Additionally, sections have been included to teach other editorial skills such as photo editing, typography, and makeup/design. These editorial skills are necessary as the student prepares to move from the classroom to communication-related jobs.

Since the first edition of this worktext, video terminals have replaced the blue pencil as the major editing tool. Pagination is a reality and newspapers are being transmitted to printing plants by satellite. While the tools may continue to change and impact certain aspects of the editing process, the fundamental concepts that produce well-edited news reports continue to be the emphasis of this book. The computer can make the editor's job easier, faster, and can even tell whether a headline fits or not, but it still takes the reporter and editor to input and correct a good news story.

The computer adage, "Garbage in, garbage out," certainly applies to news editing today. Our objective in this worktext is to provide material to develop the editing skills necessary for not only the computer age, but also for whatever age may lie ahead. Basic language skills, news judgment and headline writing still require a well-trained editor. It is our desire that this worktext will help transform the editing student into the competent editor.

The worktext is divided into 15 chapters. The chapter begins with introductory material necessary for understanding and completion of the exercises that follow. Copy for the exercises includes typical examples of news copy gathered from newspapers, TV and radio stations, student copy, plus hypothetical material. All stories contain names and places native to an average community of about 50,000 — the city of Central Valley. Appendix A contains the copy editing symbols; Appendix B has a headline schedule; Appendix C contains a map for the names of regional towns, rivers, lakes and roads; and Appendix D is a city directory for Central Valley, providing correct spelling, addresses, and occupations of the hypothetical people in the exercises (except those in datelined stories outside Central Valley).

After the student has mastered the basic editing techniques and style rules and has reviewed punctuation, grammar, and word usage rules, the next exercises introduce judgmental concepts of editing. Each exercise requires editing skills learned in previous exercises — an incremental approach.

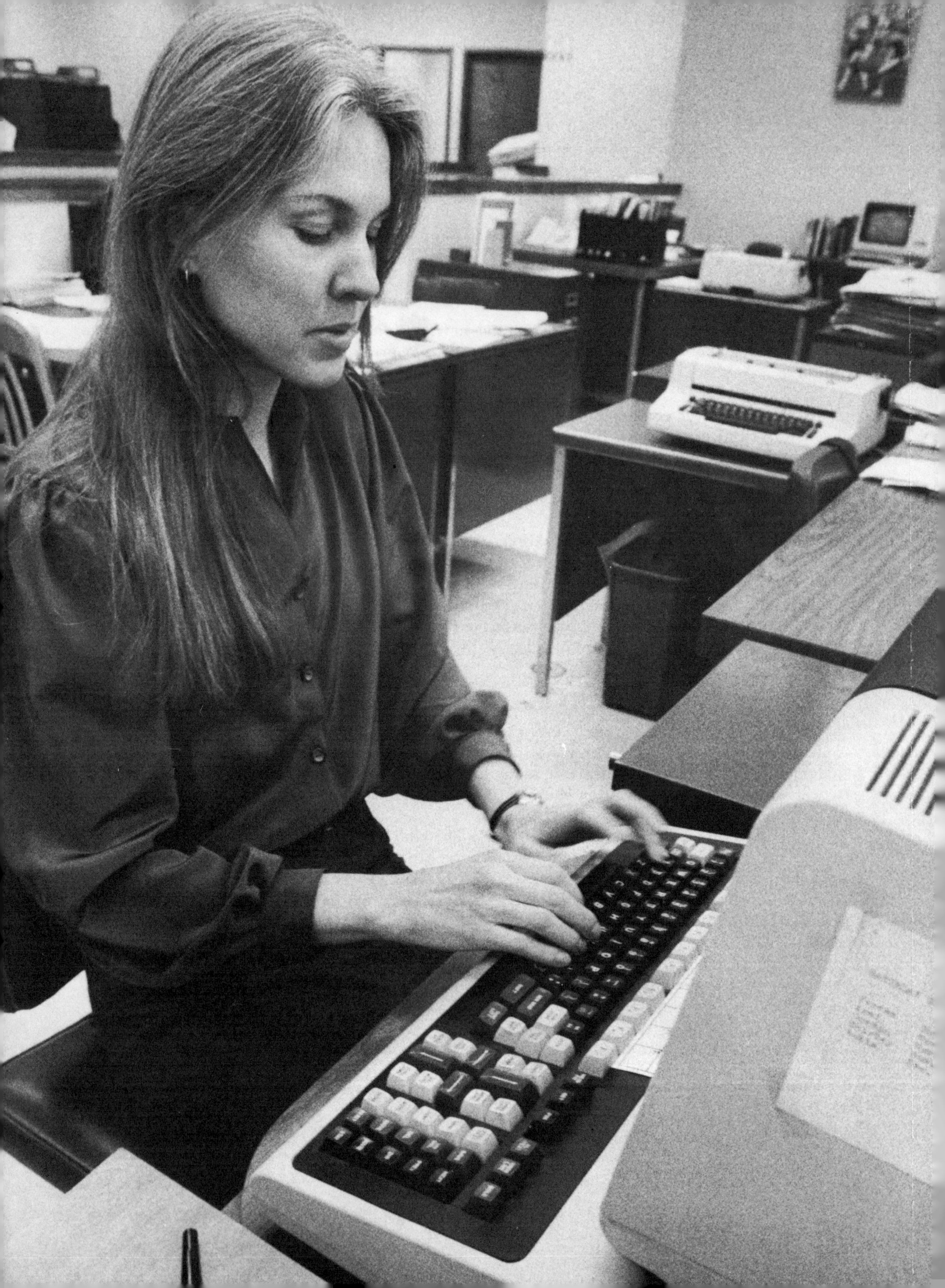

Chapter 1

The Editing Process

To understand the editorial process you first must learn how that process fits into the overall newspaper organization. Typically, the newspaper is organized into five divisions: editorial, business, advertising, production and circulation. While newspaper organization and titles vary considerably with the size of the paper, the organizational chart of a medium-sized daily often resembles this. (In Figure 1, only the editorial department is shown in detail):

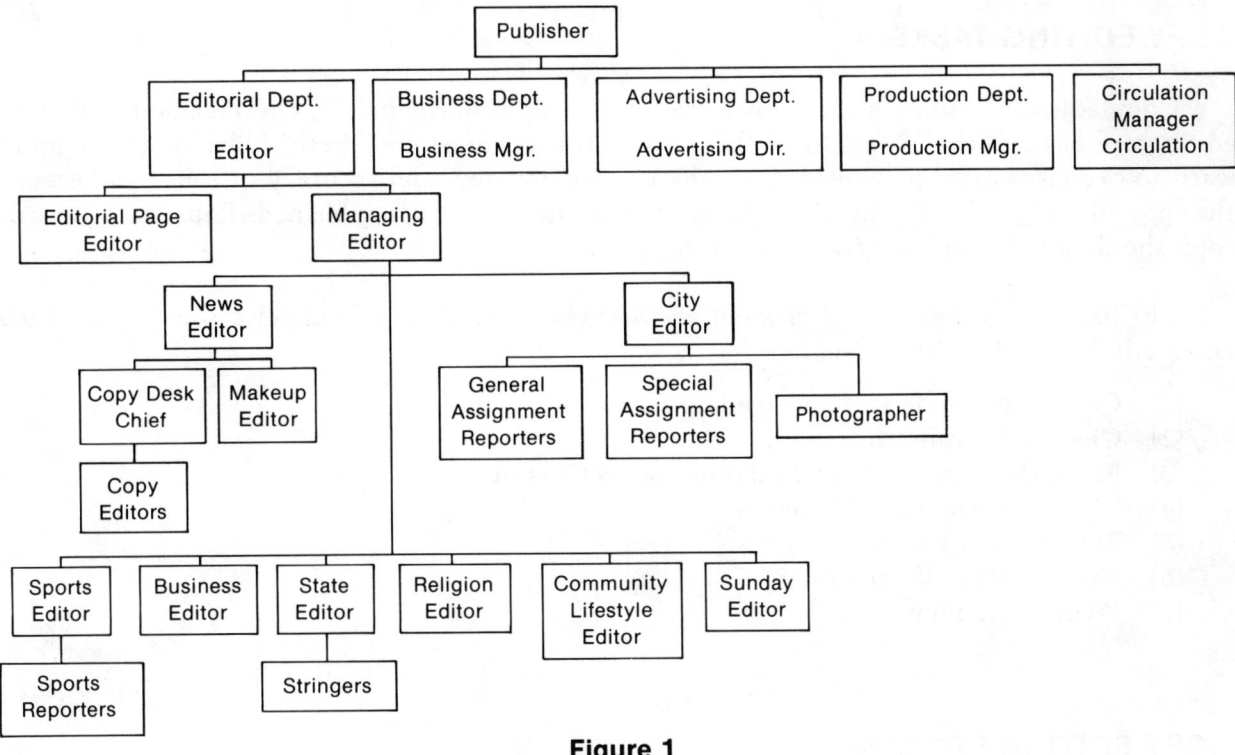

```
                                    Publisher
                                        |
    ┌───────────────┬──────────────┬────┴───────────┬──────────────┬──────────────┐
 Editorial Dept.  Business Dept.  Advertising Dept. Production Dept. Circulation
                                                                      Manager
    Editor        Business Mgr.   Advertising Dir.  Production Mgr.  Circulation
    │
    ├──────────────┐
 Editorial Page  Managing
    Editor       Editor
                    │
        ┌───────────┴───────────────────────────┐
      News                                    City
      Editor                                  Editor
        │                                      │
    ┌───┴────┐                      ┌──────────┼──────────┐
 Copy Desk  Makeup                General    Special
   Chief    Editor               Assignment  Assignment   Photographer
    │                            Reporters   Reporters
   Copy
  Editors

 ┌────────┬──────────┬────────┬──────────┬────────────┬────────┐
 Sports   Business   State    Religion   Community    Sunday
 Editor   Editor     Editor   Editor     Lifestyle    Editor
                                         Editor
   │                   │
 Sports            Stringers
 Reporters
```

**Figure 1
Newspaper Organization
Editorial Department**

The editing process is only part of the editorial department's function as you can see by the organizational chart. There are two major functions of the editorial department — reporting and editing the news. Most of the editing occurs through the news editor and the copy desk. However, each subeditor may perform some copy editing functions.

The news editor's job is the major one associated with the editing process. The news editor's responsibilities include supervision of copy editing, writing headlines and designing page makeup. It is upon the job of this subeditor and the assistants that the news editing process is focused.

THE COPY EDITOR

In order for any publication to be a professional medium it must have quality control. The copy editor is responsible for maintaining quality control. He or she reads every story prepared for the newspaper. The aim is to render every story concise, accurate and lucid. For each, the copy editor writes a headline that must give, within the rigid, unvarying space limits of type, a fair and accurate summary of the news.

The process of editing, whether for newspapers, magazines, books, or the electronic media, constitutes an important step in the communication of information. Editing can transform a dull piece of writing into a forceful presentation by rearranging the order of details, salvage a news story from a critical misstatement of fact, or save a newspaper from a libel suit.

COPY EDITING TASKS

Copy editing is much more than a mechanical skill; nevertheless, the mechanics of copy editing are basic to the editor. After the copy editor has mastered these skills, he or she must learn to exercise sound judgment about the newsworthiness and accuracy of the copy because the copy editor is normally the last editorial stop before the copy is published. Thus, each piece of copy should be read at least twice by the copy editor.

The basic tasks the copy editor must perform on a piece of unedited news copy are outlined succinctly by the *New York Times*:

(1) Correct errors in fact and spelling
(2) Check the grammar
(3) Make the copy conform to the newspaper's style
(4) Watch for libelous statements
(5) Test for news value
(6) Cut the story if necessary
(7) Write a headline

COPY EDITING PROCESS

In looking over the shoulder of the copy editor, we see the following process:

First, the copy editor draws paragraph marks to emphasize the number of paragraphs. In so doing, questions are posed to challenge the accuracy of the story. The copy editor then checks for style errors — that is, violations of the particular style adopted by the newspaper. After making any necessary changes, the copy editor places the double cross at the end of the story.

In the second reading of the story, unnecessary wording may be deleted or a fact checked. After writing a headline, the copy editor writes a slugline at the top of the story.

The total editing process, including writing the headline, takes about 10 minutes, but he has done a thorough job.

THE GATEKEEPER

The copy editor sits at the gateway between the reporter and the recipients of a news story. Whatever errors may escape the reporter, the copy editor should detect and correct. Whatever weaknesses in presentation may result from the reporter's haste or incompetence, the copy editor should challenge.

Some of the more common areas of weakness for which the copy edtor must be alert include: errors in style, errors in grammar and punctuation, errors in spelling of names and other words, weaknesses in the lead, errors of fact, inclusion of editorial comment, poor taste and libel.

COPY EDITING TASKS

Editing is a skill to improve communication. That requires improving the message for someone to read. You must have something to say to someone else, and who that someone else happens to be (your audience) helps determine how you tell (your style) what you have to say (your message).

To your considerations of audience, style and message, you should add a fourth element, purpose, to your consciousness as an editor — the question of why you are using the story, why it is important, to whom it is important, and how your story will affect those who hear it. If you can keep these four essentials of audience, style, message and purpose clear in your mind, you will immediately be a more competent editor.

Who is your audience? It's anyone's guess if you think of your audience as a faceless crowd of people. If you work for a morning daily, your audience at 7 a.m. might be made up of sleepy-heads at the breakfast table or commuters. The point is, whatever the hour of the day, your audience is not a faceless mass. Your audience is a single human being much like yourself, and it is to this single human being that you must edit. Writing to the "mass" audience, the faceless crowd, requires little commitment to communicate what others need to hear. It is much more efficient as you edit to imagine your audience as a single person who quite often is beset by distractions that lure him or her from your message, whether the distraction is a crying baby, a stoplight, the doorbell or the early morning TV news show.

TARGET AUDIENCE

Another consideration is your analysis of the newspaper's target audience, a primary bloc of readers with certain characteristics of age, economics or life style that give them a somewhat common identity. The paper then offers content calculated specifically to attract that audience.

With your audience defined, you can begin to write in a meaningful way to all those single human beings out there who are trying to listen. The story you write is your message; the way you tell it is your style. Some stories are going to be humorous; others will be deadly serious. Some will entertain; others will inform. The nature of the story, its essence, will determine your style and how you treat the story.

A modern copydesk a work in Madison, Wis. (Photo by Wisconsin State Journal.)

Name_____ **Exercise 1**

Directions: Use the proper editing symbols to correct the following sentences as instructed. See Appendix A for an example of those symbols.

1. Indicate a new paragraph for the second sentence.

    The Department will have to be reorganized according to the county treasurer. In other action, the council will seek new zoning standards for the city.

2. Indicate no paragraph.

    In other action, the council will seek new zoning standards for the city.

    New standards are needed because of the rapidly growing suburbs according to the city planner, James R. Marshall.

3. Cut out the unnecessary words.

    The mayor announced today that he will a oppose the measure.

4. Make the necessary transpositions.

    Paul Smith was named outstanding citzien.

    The ship new sunk in its inaugural voyage.

5. Make the proper correction.

    While in Pa. this summer the group will visit thirteen historical sites They will stay in 5 towns including Valley Forge, Pennsylvania.

6. Capitalize and lower case the appropriate words.

    James P. Johnson was named President of the kiwanis club.

7. Close up and separate.

    Tom Spencer died in his apart ment lastnight.

8. Retain.

    The $100 reward was presented to the student

9. Put in the appropriate punctuation marks.

    I wont run for another six year term the senator said however he will remain active in public life his wife added.

10. Center and put the following subhead in boldface.

    Sims Retains

5

Check your sentences with those below to see if you have the proper copy editing marks.

Answers

1. The department will have to be reorganized according to the county treasurer. In other action, the council will seek new zoning standards for the city.

2. In other action, the council will seek new zoning standards for the city.

    New standards are needed because of the rapidly growing suburbs according to the city planner, James R. Marshall.

3. The mayor announced today that he will a oppose the measure.

4. Paul Smith was named outstanding citzien.

5. While in Pa. this summer the group will visit thirteen historical sites. They will stay in 5 towns including Valley Forge, Pennsylvania.

6. James P. Johnson was named President of the kiwanis club.

7. Tom Spencer died in his apart ment lastnight.

8. The $100 reward was presented to the student.

9. I wont run for another six year term the senator said however he will remain active in public life his wife added

10. Sims Retains

Name_____ **Exercise 2**

Directions: Use editing symbols in the left column below to make the copy read as it is shown in the right column.

LEFT COLUMN

1. Informal agreements were reahced.
2. He refused quickly the bribe offer.
3. Collins sc ored 52 pts. in one game.
4. The tigers scoared 49 points in the last qaurter.
5. Her name is Marilynn N. Roberts.
6. She is a republican candidate.
7. Seventeen year old Joy Shea was
8. 16 college graternity brokers fought the fire, said Captian William D. Brookings.
9. It was a twenty-three minute Balloon trip across thetwon.
10. Two belligerent delinquent youngsters.

RIGHT COLUMN

Informal agreements were reached.

He quickly refused the offered bribe.

Collins scored 52 points in one game.

The Tigers scored 49 points in the last quarter.

Her name is Marilynn N. Roberts.

She is a Republican candidate.

Senior Joy Shea, 17, was

Sixteen college fraternity brothers fought the fire, Capt. William D. Brookings said.

It was a 23 minute balloon trip across the town.

Two youngsters

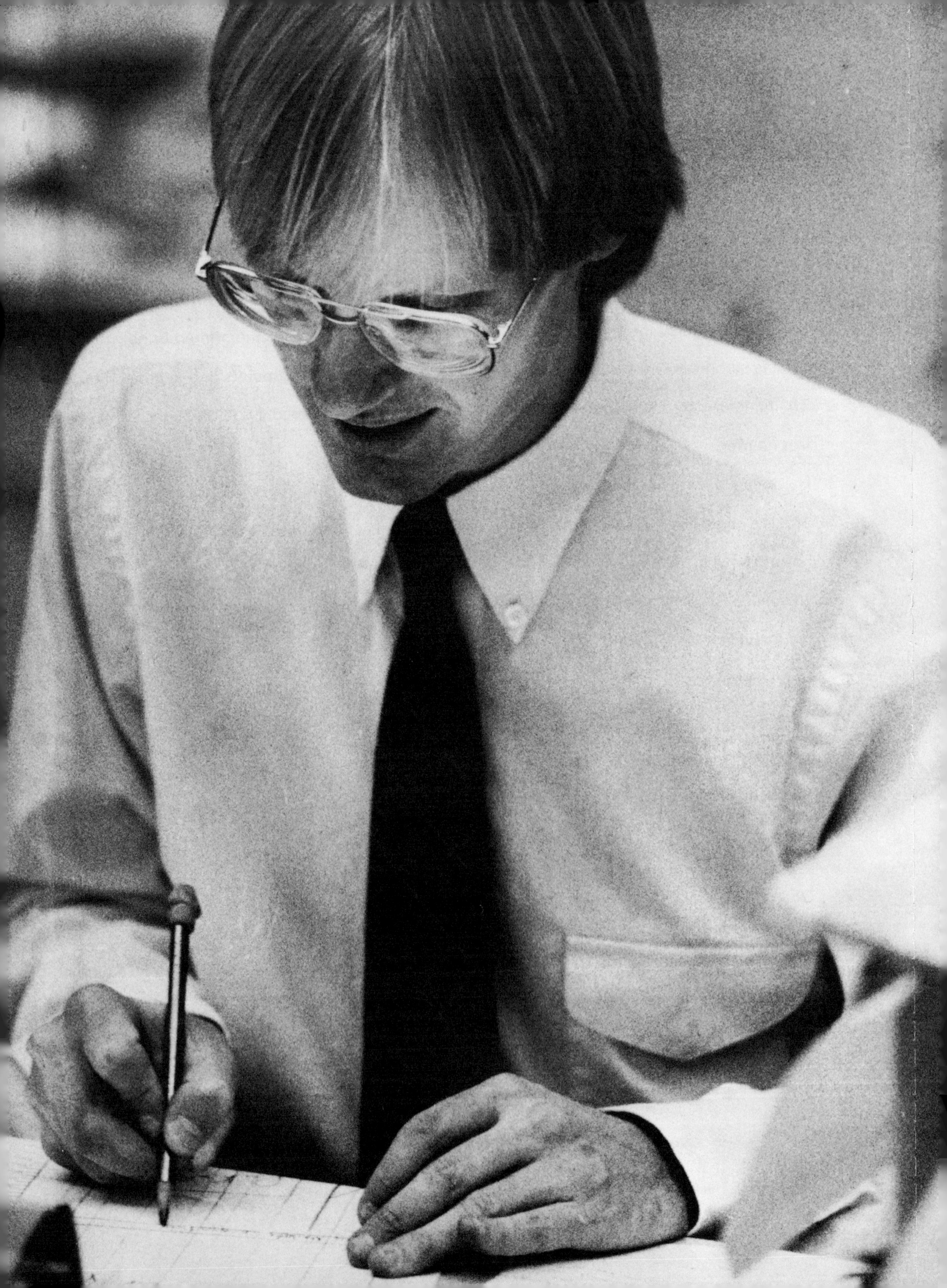

Chapter 2
News Editing Style

Style is necessary to provide consistency and to give credibility to a newspaper. There is no infallible guide to style. Instead, a thorough understanding of what it is, what the principal rules are, and how it should be applied is necessary if it is to work for, instead of against, a newspaper's credibility.

Writing style is thought of in two ways: personal style or mechanical style. Our concern is not so much the personal style except that it conforms to the overall style of conciseness, logic, and simplicity. Journalistic style is usually referred to as mechanical style. Mechanical style concerns such matters as punctuation, abbreviation, spelling, and capitalization.

Style evolves to meet the needs of the communicator to be consistent in the communication message. Today most journalistic style is governed by the extensive style books produced by the two major wire services, United Press International and Associated Press. Each came out with a separate style guide in 1978, but with only a few minor exceptions the guides are the same. The 1978 version was put together by a joint committee of the wire services.

Copy editors must know the style books well enough to either know a particular rule regarding a capitalization problem or a punctuation question, or at least to know where to find the rule rapidly. Unfortunately, the style guides do not cover every possible style problem. Occasionally a newspaper editor must decide for that newspaper. These style issues usually are appended to the newspaper's style guides.

Besides capitalization, punctuation, abbreviations, and spelling there are other style issues that are important to you as the editor. These include checking for accuracy, attribution words, updating the story and localizing it.

ACCURACY

One of the essential qualities of fair reporting is accuracy. No newspaper can maintain an image of journalistic integrity if news reports are consistently inaccurate. Missed facts, inaccuracies, distortions of emphasis — all damage your credibility.

Inadequacies, half-truths and inconsistencies all raise questions in reader's minds about the possibility of biased reporting. Traditionally, journalism has even come under attack for fair reporting. When your accuracy and fairness are above reproach, some will still castigate you for reporting what happened, and others will chastise you for not reporting what happened.

Given the nature of journalism, all this is natural and to be expected. Anyone in the news, whether public official or labor union leader, wants to be shown in a favorable light. Accurate reporting demands that you show people as they are, whether good or bad, and "let the chips fall where they may" when it comes to the impact and effect of your reporting. It will never be your role as a journalist to tell people what they would like to hear; it will be your job to edit the story as accurately as you can, even when the facts are unpleasant.

Accuracy demands much of you. In even the simplest stories, you will have to check and recheck the smallest details, verify that names, ages and addresses are complete and accurate; you will have to determine whether streets and rivers run in the directions that wire services and fellow writers claim; you will have to ascertain whether your use of statistics is fair or misleading; and you will have to find out whether "yesterday" in Paris is still "today" in the United States. If you are diligent in your commitment to honest, accurate reporting, your audience will trust you; it will seek out your newspaper as a professional information source.

On a more personal level, accuracy is vitally important to newspeople for other reasons — inaccuracy is one way to lose your job or subject yourself and your newspaper to costly lawsuits.

ATTRIBUTION

As a journalist, you should never take responsibility for predicting the future or vouch for the accuracy of statements you cannot substantiate. Be on the alert for statements that must be attributed such as the following:

1. Sodium phenobarbital injections provide a more humane way to dispose of pets than compression chambers.
2. Abortion is a return to primitive, barbaric values.
3. Continued imports of foreign oil will drive America bankrupt.
4. The gasoline shortage will cause many independent retailers to go out of business.
5. Carlson will withdraw as the nominee for highway director.

If you look again at the statements above, you can easily identify their controversial nature. As a journalist, why should you assume responsibility for reporting such information as gospel fact?

Example 1 calls for attribution to an expert, someone with qualifications to state as fact that sodium phenobarbital injections are more humane than other pet disposal methods.

Statement 2 is an emotion-laden value judgment; either you must attribute the statement to a source or label your story as personal comment or an editorial.

Statement 3 places you in the position of crystal-gazer unless you attribute. Who says foreign oil imports will drive America bankrupt? Tell your audience who made the statement, then let your audience judge for itself the accuracy of the statement and the integrity of the source.

Statement 4 begs attribution in a similar way. Did an independent gasoline retailer make the statement, or did an economist or politician? Tell your audience.

Statement 5 fails to include the source as an essential part of the story. Only Mr. Carlson could decide to withdraw his name from nomination, so tell your audience that the source of the story made the announcement.

ATTRIBUTION WORDS

When you write any story that requires attribution, you may be tempted to try word substitutes for the familiar "said," as used in the following example:

Scientists said the new pill may cause liver damage.

"Said," as used in this example, is a neutral verb. It places no value of any kind upon the statement that follows. Equally neutral are the words "told" and "reported," which simply relate an act of communication without imposing any value on the statement communicated:

Scientists told reporters the new pill may cause liver damage.

Scientists reported the new pill may cause liver damage.

Beyond this point, attribution words begin to impose an editorial flavor to your writing because they tend to change the story's meaning.

Be particularly alert to changes in meaning when using the following words:

WARNED	ASSERTED
DECLARED	CONTINUED
ADDED	POINTED OUT
VOWED	DISCLOSED
STATED	PROMISED

The subtle changes in meaning become apparent when you substitute these words for the more neutral "said," "told," or "reported."

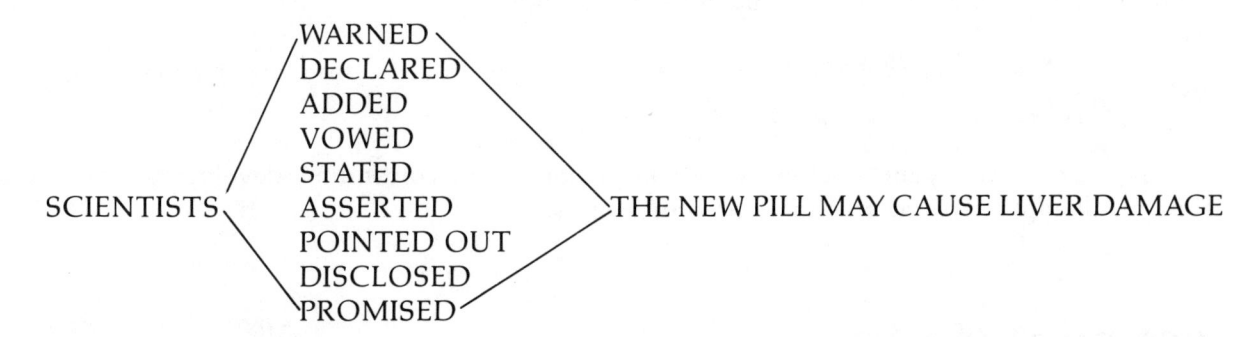

SCIENTISTS [WARNED / DECLARED / ADDED / VOWED / STATED / ASSERTED / POINTED OUT / DISCLOSED / PROMISED] THE NEW PILL MAY CAUSE LIVER DAMAGE

In the example above, WARNED is an acceptable word for attribution, but DECLARED sounds pompous. ADDED indicates that the possibility of liver damage was given as an afterthought. VOWED is too strong because it implies a pomposity beyond the scientist's original intent. STATED is stiff and formal. ASSERTED sounds as if the writer is challenging the scientists' statement. POINTED OUT makes the statement sound as if it is secondary or peripheral. DISCLOSED makes the statement sound as if the scientists had exclusive information just now being made public, and PROMISED sounds more dire than the scientists may have intended the statement to be. Clearly, each word imparts a slightly different context to the information.

UPDATE YOUR STORIES

Some news that you report will be in the nature of on-going, evolving stories and will have to be updated each time new developments occur. A generous application of common sense is your best guide in knowing when to update a story. In general, however, you should update a story every time new information occurs.

The reasons for updating are obvious. You are in the business of reporting news (new developments) and should pass along this new information to your audience at the earliest opportunity.

Imagine a downtown fire in which a business is destroyed and damage has reached an estimated $350,000.

Your 5 a.m. story might be:

> Firemen are battling a two-alarm fire in the downtown business district.

By 10 a.m., when the fire is out, your lead for the next edition might be:

> Investigators are trying to learn what caused the fire that destroyed a downtown business during the night.

By noon, your lead for the early afternoon edition might be:

> Damage is estimated at $350,000 in the aftermath of a fire that destroyed a downtown business early this morning.

Your lead at 2 p.m. for your final edition might be:

> Arson is suspected in the two-alarm fire that destroyed a downtown business early today.

Always lead with your most up-to-date information in a continuing, developing story. Your readers will appreciate the freshness of your stories.

LOCALIZING

> State Senator Richard Long is among those attending a national legislative conference today in Washington.

A lead similar to the one above gives readers in your region reason to become interested in an otherwise national story. You should search for local tie-ins to national stories whenever possible.

Localize your stories whenever it is natural and possible. Search for the local angles to regional and national events. Help your audience relate to news whenever it is happening.

HARD VS. SOFT NEWS

The two most classical distinctions between news are between hard news, and soft, or feature news.

Hard news is what people expect to hear. It is the news they need to know to get along in life from day to day, news that helps them decide which course of action to take or that affects them financially, physically or in some other important way. Hard news tells about rate hikes in utilities, property tax increases, important Senate action, or of major crime in the community.

Soft news is optional to news the audience might enjoy hearing but could live without, such as a report on how a local television newswoman learns to belly dance, how more firemen are growing beards these days, how the Rhode Island man who pushes a peanut up the sidewalk to pay off an election bet, or how local school teachers are exercising three times a week until semester's end. Such stories may contribute to our awareness of social or community trends or to our understanding of how events affect us. If they serve any of these functions they are justified, but not if they replace stories we need to know.

SPOT NEWS

A spot news story is an event that breaks out, day or night, without warning. You may find yourself covering a variety of spot news — the fires, holdups, car wrecks, plane crashes, drownings and murders that occur from time to time in almost any community. Gradually you will learn that the news never changes. Only the names change. The same stories return day after day, year after year.

Such stories are often accounts of violence, and they will leave some people in your audience cold. Still others in your audience will be interested in such events. Your audience may have witnessed a car-train collision and will be eager to learn what happened. Others in your audience may be vitally interested in hearing about the third holdup in as many days at the mom and pop grocery just down the street from where they live.

Some spot news is momentous: a million dollar warehouse fire, a major drug raid, a train derailment, flash flooding, and grain elevator explosions are examples. Other spot news barely qualifies for the title and needs unusual angles to make it newsworthy.

In general, as you make judgments about spot news, you should ask yourself what lifts the story out of the ordinary. Why waste precious space reporting minor-injury accidents, inconsequential fires, and $25 holdups?

Many editors are satisfied covering only WHAT of events. Others will go beyond surface coverage whenever possible and ask WHY events occurred and what CONSEQUENCES are likely. Such questions help the editor probe for the cause of stories. This is not to imply that you should become a crusading journalist, only that you should go beyond the symptom of a problem (the grain elevator explosion) and get to the cause (lax safety standards that surround the handling of grain dust). Only when people are aware of problems can the causes be addressed.

REFERENCE SOURCES

Tools of the editor include reference materials, and no newsroom should be without at least the minimum references:

— Style guides are the basic reference sources for the editor. An AP and UPI guide are both necessary as are any local news guides that may have been specifically prepared for your paper.

— City directories help locate people, their addresses and telephone numbers. People not listed in normal telephone directories may be found in the city directory. This reference is especially useful when you are trying to contact someone near the scene of a fire or accident for eyewitness information. Most city directories also provide cross sections by name, address and telephone number. This makes it possible for you to locate someone even if you know only the address or telephone number and are unsure of the name.

— Out-of-town telephone directories help you locate people and agencies outside your immediate area.

— Unlisted telephone numbers and other numbers that are frequently called can be listed to speed the reporting process. A file of such numbers contains many which aren't listed in the phone book — a police dispatcher's private line, for instance — and which may be unavailable from other sources on a moment's notice. Caution: don't give out unlisted numbers to anyone except those who are authorized to use them.

— Public officials and agencies make up another reference source which should list position held, political affiliation, pertinent telephone numbers, political record of official involved, function of agency and the like. Most states have a "Blue Book" directory which lists Congressmen and women by name, party, terms held, office address and telephone number. Such directories are helpful when you must quickly learn as much as possible about a public official.

— Directories are, of course, indispensable to any writer. Besides an up-to-date dictionary, you may want a dictionary of synonyms, a thesaurus, and even a book of famous quotations as a stimulus on days when you suffer from uninspired writing.

— Other newspapers and news magazines help you keep abreast of local, regional, state, national and international news. Most newsrooms subscribe to local and state newspapers and at least one or two news magazines.

— Newsroom radio monitors and television monitors to help keep tabs on the broadcast media and as a check against your news coverage. Monitoring the competition keeps you alert to any stories you may have missed in the day's news coverage.

Name_____   **Exercise 3**

REFERENCE EXERCISE

Directions: Give answers and sources of information for these questions using the most recent source. Give the source for the information.

1. Who were the leading players in "Camelot," a 1968 movie?
2. Who is the editor of the Watseka, Ill. Times-Republic?
3. Who is the city editor of the Kansas City Star?
4. How much salary is paid the governor of Nevada?
5. Who is president of Baylor University?
6. How many daily newspapers are published in California? Which one is the smallest in terms of circulation?
7. What is the circulation of Time magazine?
8. What is the name of the University of Texas newspaper?
9. Who was the vice president during Grover Cleveland's second term?
10. Who is the attorney general of Wisconsin?
11. Who won and what was the score of the 1970 Davis Cup matches?
12. Address a letter to the secretary of the American Oriental Society.
13. When and where was Woodrow Wilson born?
14. When was New Mexico admitted to the Union?
15. What is the area of El Salvador (in square miles)?
16. What is the steamship distance (in nautical miles) from San Francisco to Honolulu?
17. Who is the mayor of San Francisco?
18. What is the average wind speed at Salt Lake City?
19. Of what state is Sen. John Tower a senator?
20. How many Congressional districts are there in New York state?
21. What is the record low temperature for Colorado and when and where was it recorded?
22. Who is the mayor of New Orleans, La.?

Name_____   **Exercise 4**

ABBREVIATIONS

Directions: Style rules on abbreviations are difficult to learn because of the numerous exceptions and inconsistencies. Completing the following exercise should familiarize you with some of the rules and exceptions, but there will always be many more that are impossible to cover here. Put either **abbreviated** or **written out** in the blank provided unless a specific answer is called for. Use your stylebook as a guide.

1. If there is not an exact street number given, street, avenue, boulevard and terrace are _____. However, if there is an exact address, they are _____.

2. Other components of addresses such as port, circle, drive, lane, are always _____.

3. _____ states which follow cities. However, with the exception of Texas, only states of more than six letters are _____.

4. All states that stand alone are _____.

5. Titles before names should be capitalized and _____, but titles following names are _____. An exception would be the president. President is never _____ when referring to the head of the United States government.

6. Most names of organizations are _____ the first time, and then _____ in subsequent references.

7. _____ months of five letters or more when used in dates, but _____ when there is no accompanying date. The year makes no difference in whether the months are written our or abbreviated.

8. Days of the week are _____.

9. Periods are used most of the time in lower case abbreviations. Thus, collect on delivery would be abbreviated _____.

10. _____ the mountain and army post, but _____ the city. Thus, Fort Collins, Colorado, would be written _____.

17

Name_____   **Exercise 5**

CAPITALIZATION

Directions: Most print media use a modified "down style" — they capitalize as infrequently as possible. The reasons for the capitalization style rules are not always known or apparent, and must sometimes be followed simply because that is the rule. The only general rule governing capitalization is that proper names are capitalized.

Using your stylebook as a guide, complete the following exercise.

Put in the blank either **capitalize** or **lower case.**

1. _____ titles preceding a name. _____ titles that stand alone or follow a name.
2. _____ occupational or false titles.
3. _____ U.S. Congress, Senate, House.
4. _____ City Council when used without the city name.
5. _____ the state legislature when preceded by the state name.
6. _____ The exact title of any organization.
7. _____ all words within an exact title except articles, conjunction "and," and prepositions of five letters or less.
8. Military branches are _____ whether their title is exact or not.
9. _____ the names of courts.
10. _____ the names of political parties and _____ the word "party."
11. _____ direction. _____ specific regions.
12. All direct references to the Deity are _____. Pronouns referring to the Deity are _____. Sacred writings of religions are _____.
13. The names of races and nationalities are _____. The reference by color is a common name and therefore _____.
14. _____ common noun when it is part of the formal name. _____ the common noun when standing alone.
15. _____ titles of books, songs, poems, etc., and place quotation marks.
16. _____ the first word of a quotation making a complete sentence. _____ the first word of a quotation if the sentence is incomplete.
17. _____ specific names of species of animals.
18. _____ holidays such as Labor Day, Christmas.

Name_____   **Exercise 6**

NUMERALS

Directions: The style for numerals is easy to remember. In general, write out all numbers below 10 and put all others in numerical form. The problem, though, is that there are numerous exceptions to the general rule.

The reason for using numerals in writing include saving space and enhancing clarity. Therefore, when in doubt about whether or not to put the number as a figure, it is probably safer to do so.

Do the following exercise to help learn the basic rule and some of the exceptions using your stylebook as a guide.

1. You should write out numbers _____ through _____.

2. To begin a sentence with a number you should _____.
   (write out, put in figures)

3. Use numbers _____ for ages, heights, dates, and addresses.
   (as general rule, exclusively)

4. Use numbers _____ in statistical matter, records, elections, speeds,
   (as general rule, exclusively)
   highways, distances, dimensions, and temperatures.

5. While addresses are _____, the specific street follows the
   (written out, as figures)
   _____.
   (general rule, exception)

6. While ages for man and animal are _____, they are
   (written out, figures)
   _____ for inanimate objects.
   (written out, figures)

7. Per cent follows the _____ and is _____
   (general rule, exception)   (always a numeral,
   _____.
   both numeral and written out depending on general rule)

8. In a series of numbers you should _____.
   (write out, use figures, use simplest form)

9. Fractions or decimals used with a whole number are _____, but
   (written out, figures)
   fractions alone are _____.
   (written out, figures)

10. Casual numbers are _____ (written out, figures). Thus, "A _____ (1000, thousand) times no!"

11. Money is _____ (written out, figures) except when dealing with cents alone, then it _____ (follows general rule, uses figures). Thus five dollars would be written _____ and five cents _____.

12. Numerals combined with the word number are _____ (written out, figures).

    Thus, the number one candidate would be written No. _____ candidate.

13. Time is _____ (in figures, written out) except for noon and midnight which must be _____ (written out, figures) following the _____ (figure, word) twelve.

14. Highway numbers are _____ (written out, figures). They will be at the intersection of U.S. _____ (nine, 9) and Interstate _____ (ninety, 90).

15. In amounts of more than a million you usually round off the number and carry to _____ (one, two) decimal places if needed. You write out million or billion, but you put the exact amount in numerals. If you do not round off the number, then it is written entirely as a numerals. Therefore, two million six hundred thousand forty would be _____, if you round off the numbers. The $ sign is equivalent to the second numeral; therefore, with all numbers using the dollar sign you use figures. The number three million dollars would be written _____ and three million persons _____.

22

Name_____   **Exercise 7**

PUNCTUATION EXERCISE

Directions: Edit the following sentences to conform with Associated Press style. Correct all errors, including typographical and spelling.

1. The captain went with me to the lake and he helped me find the camp.
2. The following have the information Tom Paul Helen and George.
3. Sarahs new microwave oven includes many new features, touch programing, defrosting, and delay set.
4. The man, who lives next door, works at Hewlett-Packard.
5. He wrote a 500 page book however it was about 200 pages too long.
6. Because each employee has a certain type of work to do each day the plant manager must arrange work schedules to meet both the plant and employee objectives.
7. Our ofice will be moved but the new location hasnt been decided.
8. The instrument has a dual function to increase gasoline and to regulate emissions.
9. Harold Red Grange asked the question will the Cowboys win tomorrow.
10. The speech entitled To Live or Die was given by the editor of Christianity Today but tomorrows lecture will be presented by Paul Rogers editor of the Central Valley Free Press.
11. He said "I will give up tomorrow; but he didn't.
12. The 9 year old boy will be taken to the hospital consequently his mother will have to find a baby-sitter for her older son Joe.
13. Tom Rue managing editor, is responsible for meeting the 1030 a m deadline and for the page make-up.
14. Paul Smith of Dallas said "We ought to fire Paul Slim Slaughter treasurer of Jones and Co., he hasnt worked three days this month".
15. If the pictures come in today we will be able to publish the magazine on time however if they don't we will be a week later because the printer has other commitments for the rest of the week.

16. Gov Jones 45 was reelected to the job by 2101 votes and he will take a vacation to Hawaii to celebrate.

17. National Education Association (NEA) will sue the state of New York for violation of teachers rights in the strike.

18. Prof Sam Adams of Adams State predicts this years election will draw 65 percent of voters to the polls (the largest turnout in 10 years).

19. However election officials believe only 40 percent of the voters will turnout for the election (It would be the smallest turnout in six years).

20. He will go but wont like it Tom Smith said referring to his client Ralph Smith Jr.

Name_____ **Exercise 8**

Directions: Edit the following sentences to conform with Associated Press Style. You need to use the proper copyreading symbols, and correct all errors. You should look particularly for style errors involving capitalization and abbreviation.

1. Robert L. Jones of the Italian republican army said that "the day of victory is near."

2. The question came up: What to do.

3. The United States sentate passed the bill.

4. "Let's go have a coke," he said.

5. The girl scouts held a meeting yesterday.

6. The Lions Club of Central Valley elected the following officers: J. D. Collins, Pres.; Harry Lewis, vice-pres.; William Kelly, Secretary; and Kenneth Harris Jr., Treasuer.

7. No one won the nobel peace prize the nobel peace prize this year.

8. A traffic accident occured on Central Valley south side.

9. Ohio is called the buckeye state.

10. "Now and in time" is opening here tomorrow.

11. Rain fell in the southern part of the state yesterday.

12. The black race is striving for equality em;ployment.

13. Robert is a member of the Republican party.

14. The residents of 120 South Avenue, 43 East Homewood St., 171 Lavalette Rd and 151 Woodland Ter were robbed on the same night.

15. Rookie left-handed Pitcher Bill Miles willy marry the daughter of Defense Attorney John Jones.

16. The traffic accident occurred on South Main Street about a block from his home at 16 East State Street.

17. Woods is employed by the english department.

18. The city council granted his request.

19. William Froome is President of the Central Valley board of education.

20. Secy. of State Edward Grace and Atty. Gen. Robert Munson planned to meet Tues., but had to shift their meeting to Thur.

21. R. C. Harris jr. was the first negro to represent the US Government in that position.

22. The hearing has been set for wednesday by judge Richard Zem in the case of a local couple who pleaded inocent in city cout today on charges of running a red light and speeding.

23. willy and willa schlonck, 3232 lincoln rd., were cited by ptim anthony Casamassima, early this morning.

24. He reported they were racing their fiat sports car in circles around the traffic light at Wheeling avenue and red river boulevard.

25. Willy schlonck, 3232 lincoln shire, said the top prize of a years' social security payments would be awarded to the winner.

Name_____ **Exercise 9**

Directions: Edit the following sentences to conform with Associated Press style. Correct all errors, including typographical and spelling.

1. Station KCVU originats from Central Valley University.

2. "I recall that year", he said in reference to when the state budget was 78,200,000 dollars.

3. The number one candidate spent almost three million dollars during his campaign for the United States sentate position.

4. The most unique gift a brass foot-warmer she recieved from her grandfather and grandmother.

5. Hurricane jane threatens the cotton state, Misissippi.

6. He was born at a time when World War one was as fresh in the minds of some men as Vietnam is to some men today.

7. Tenn-agers will collect for the United Way appeal again this year he noted.

8. The Russia spokesman said that communism is the only true form of government for people living in the far east.

9. Bruce W. O'Brien, of Plains City, was serious injured in a fire which destroyed his house at 62 Sixth Street.

10. The housing project sets out to improve living conditions increase convenience in location and a decrease in neighborhood vandalizing.

11. Professor Tom J. Smith is the author of a new text, The New Journalism.

12. The nine year old girl was one of the seventy-sic persons who arrived before 8:00 p.m.

13. His book is titled "The Loser".

14. The question came up: what should he do now.

15. He asked the question, 'why does the federal government require income tax payment every year?'

16. "What is going on here," he asked?

17. Another fireworks display will be featured the day after the 4th of July to celebrate the one hundred anniversary of Central Valley.

18. The ariplane achieved a speed of 2,400 mph, though it was only expected to travel at 1,600 mph.

19. A person like you who pays their subscription promptly is the backbone of American magazines.

20. The publishers disagreed and has to meet again.

21. Referring to our telephone interview yesterday, the information you requested for are enclosed.

22. Concluding that this press was a poor risk, the question was submitted to the business office for decision.

23. A smaller staff might be appropriate for handling the regular volume of correspondance but not a larger one.

24. Will you please let us know who sent you the original tip to since it apparently was not received at the newsroom.

25. Everybody in our radio station want to express their appreciation to you for your thoughtfulness.

Name_____ **Exercise 10**

Directions: Edit the story.

The Rhode Island court of appeals has figured out a way to cut down on it's backlog of cases by adding judges — and it didnt even need to get legislativ authorization.

Later this month of January, it will create a 4th devision composed of a couple of retired judges and the current chief judge of the court.

theyll put in sixty working days a year for the hearing of new cases so the regular court members can rule on the cases they already have.

The new appellate devision will be paid for out of existing budget for socalled sr. judges who for several years have filled in on district courts.

Directions: Edit the story.

CHICAGO — 17 people have been arrested in a mult-million $ cocaine ring. Children's book were used to smuggle the drug in the United states from South America.

These illegal packages containing hidden drugs were delivered Friday by federal postal inspectors dressed as mail carriers. They were accompanioned by local officers of the police and federal agents, said Joan Ryle, commander of the narcotics section of the Chicago Police Department's Organized Crime Unit.

As soon as a recipient signed for the package, the police arrested him or her, Ryle added.

More than twenty lbs. of cocaine was seized in fifteen different locations during the arrests on Friday, Ryle said.

The arrests and seizures took place in Chicago and four suburbs.

###

Name_____ **Exercise 11**

Directions: Edit the story.

New York — The worst storm in yrs. left the Northeast a winter no-man's land Mon. and closed schools, airports, highways, and businesses.

As the death toll mounts, Mt. Vernon, New York appear to be the hardest hit. The death count reached twenty-five in the Mt. Vernon area. The total reached forty-seven in storm-connected deaths across New York and the New England states.

Authorities said the digging out process would take until the end of the week in some localities where wind-whipped drifts crested at at more than 6 ft. Major Chas. H. White of Saint James, N.Y. banned at travled in his city.

The U.N. cancelled all of their meetings. The N.Y. and American stock exchange were closed for the day for the second time in their history.

Hardship was incalculable as the result of the greatest accumulation of snow since January 12, 1961. The storm in January of 1961, dumped accumulations of up to eight ft. of snow on upper New York. Saint John, New Brunswick, was paralized for two weeks during the 1961 storm which left 67 dead.

###

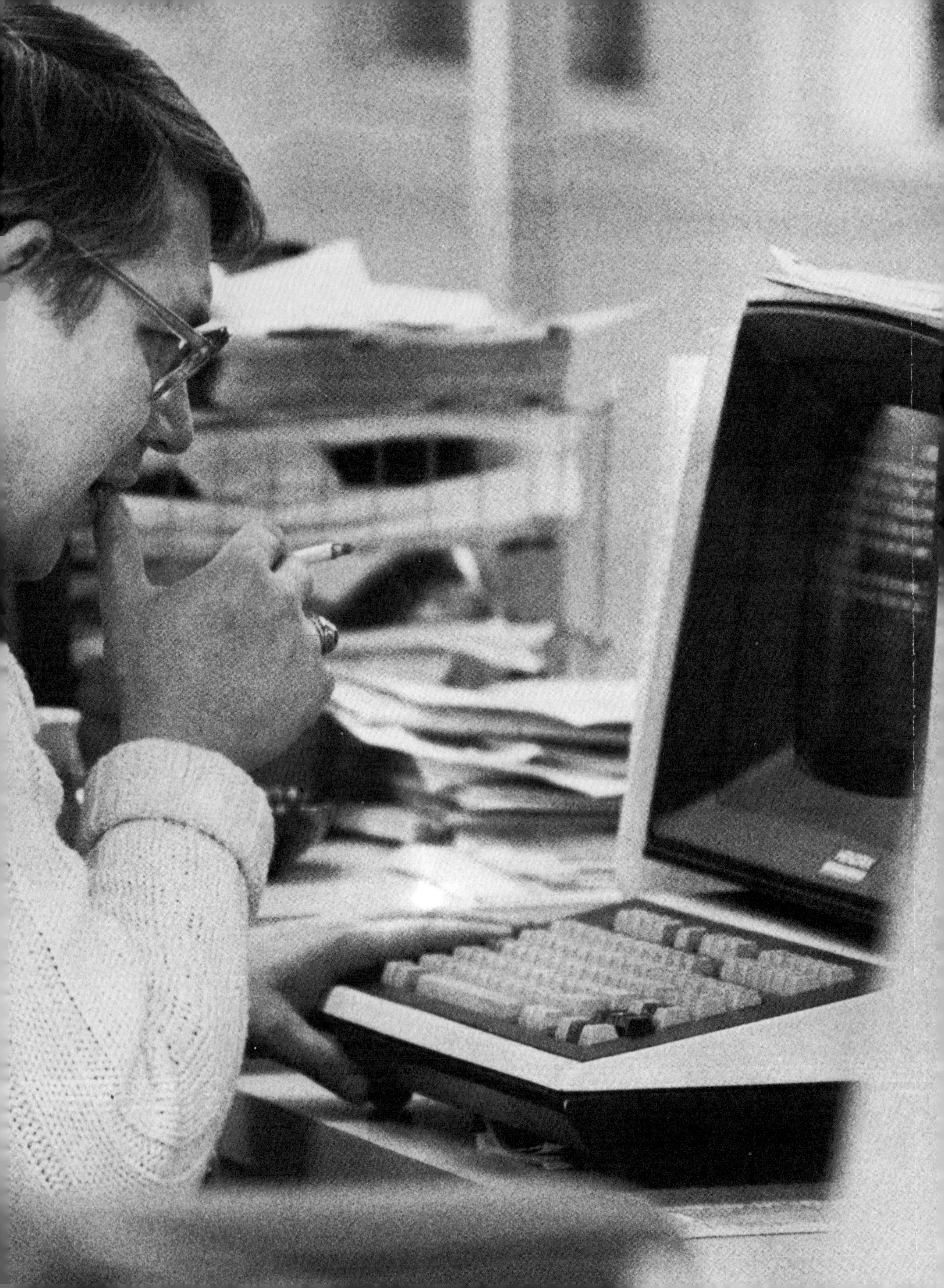

Chapter 3
Language Usage

The challenge to the copy editor is to improve an often mediocre news story to one that will be not only mechanically perfect, but also will be crisp, interesting, and inviting to the reader. To do this requires a love for the language and its exactness. Correct verb tense, voice, word usage, and grammar all play a significant role in making the news story interesting, but brevity adds the crispness to it.

BREVITY

Edit, but edit carefully to achieve brevity and style in a news story.

As a beginning copy editor, your biggest problem is what to edit. You may forget that a news story is told in short sentences and paragraphs, and in the past tense. Additionally, your choice of verbs should be active ones, such as ordered, denied or praised, instead of was, were or has, the easiest verbs to use in writing but the most unappealing.

Editors achieve brevity by applying what they know about news writing. They utilize the news concept of a single idea in a sentence, and apply length variations for sentences and paragraphs in a story. They prefer one common word, rather than two or three sophisticated words for the same thought.

Editors, in reading a news story for the first time, do not assume that conciseness in a story merely means deleting the last paragraphs. Instead, they read the story looking for "glittering generalities," "cliches," stock phrases, and other story padding that isolates the major facts. Sometimes story padding comes in the form of dangling modifiers and superlatives, and in other instances in simple sentences that add little, if anything, to an article. You should watch for verbal phrases which can be reduced to a single verb. For example, you can shorten "try an experiment" to "experiment" or "made an appearance" to "appeared."

Copy editors know that most of the "hard news" story types, such as government stories, tend to confuse the reader rather than inform him. As a result, they should give extra attention to simplicity in these stories.

By following the idea that journalistic writing is writing to communicate, not impress, you should see the importance of keeping stories short, but readable. Here are some ways to do so:

1. ELIMINATE CLICHES, STOCK PHRASES, GLITTERING GENERALITIES.

    He traveled ~~a distance of~~ 12 miles.

    One of the ~~most outstanding~~ former mayors . . .

2. SHORTEN VERBAL PHRASES TO SIMPLE VERBS.

    He ~~made~~ mention*ed* ~~of~~ the new contract in today's speech.

3. DELETE UNNECESSARY WORDS OR PHRASES.

    Roger W. Murray paid ~~in the neighborhood of~~ *about* $80,000 for his home.

4. ELIMINATE REPETITION OR REDUNDANCY.

    The club will meet ~~for its regular monthly meeting~~ tomorrow at 3 p.m. in the auditorium.

5. USE SIMPLE WORDS FOR CLARITY.

    He ~~substantiated~~ *checked* the facts.

VERB TENSE

Newspapers traditionally report the news in past tense. Feature material often uses the present tense. News sounds more current and dynamic if you report in the present tense: Police say two persons are being questioned . . . The White House tonight reports new developments in the controversial question of . . . Firemen are battling a two-alarm fire that broke out late tonight . . .

Let's look at some other examples.

PRESENT TENSE: Striking coal workers hope a settlement can be reached tonight.
PAST PERFECT TENSE: Striking coal workers were reported hopeful a settlement could be reached tonight. (Is there a chance they are still hopeful?)
PAST TENSE: Striking coal workers hoped a settlement could be reached tonight.

Notice how the shift in tense subtly changes the meaning of the story and how, as you shift from present to past tense, the immediacy of the story is lost. Look especially at the sentence written in past tense. It sounds somewhat negative about hopes for a settlement. Present tense offers an additional benefit — it helps keep sentences shorter. Sometimes present tense will sound awkward and artificial. If it does, don't hesitate to switch to past tense or to past perfect tense.

ACTIVE vs. PASSIVE VOICE

Excessive use of passive voice often demonstrates lazy thinking. Active voice, by contrast, results in more understandable copy, shorter sentences and dynamic expression. The differences are easy to distinguish:

If the subject of the verb receives the action, the verb is in the passive voice.

> The burglar was shot three times by police.

If the subject of a verb is the doer of the action, the verb is in the active voice:

> Police shot the burglar three times.

While active voice generally is more lively, specific and concise, passive voice is useful to place emphasis on the object of the action. Notice in the passive voice example that emphasis is placed on the burglar (the object of the action), while in the active voice example, emphasis is placed on the police (the doer of the action).

WORD USAGE

The editor draws from a full, varied vocabulary, rich in specific words that convey exact meaning and connotation. The editor understands differences in words for particular situations. For example, the word "government" is more neutral than the word "regime." If a word has more than one meaning, it is used in the correct context to avoid confusion. Consideration of the audience must be involved in the journalist's examination of word usage in the news story.

Generally, it is preferable to use the simple word rather than the complex, the concrete instead of the abstract, and the active rather than the passive voice. Avoid slang, foreign words, highly technical words or phrases, and cliches.

The following list of words and phrases is provided to indicate word usage preferred by journalists.

1. ACCEPT, EXCEPT. ACCEPT means to receive, while EXCEPT as a verb means to exclude, and as a preposition, EXCEPT means with the exception of.
2. AFFECT, EFFECT. AFFECT usually is the verb; EFFECT is the noun. However, EFFECT may be a verb when it means to bring about.
3. AFTERWARD, AFTERWARDS. Use AFTERWARD rather than AFTERWARDS. The same rule applied to TOWARD.
4. AGREE TO, AGREE WITH. You AGREE TO a proposed action and you AGREE WITH someone.
5. AGGREGATE. Do not use when meaning total. It's not a substitute for total, but means a group of distinct things gathered together.

6. ALLUDE, ELUDE. You ALLUDE to a movie (mention indirectly), and you ELUDE a tackler (escape).
7. AMONG, BETWEEN. Use AMONG when more than two are meant. Use BETWEEN with two only.
8. ANNUAL. If it is the first time, it cannot be ANNUAL.
9. AVERSE, ADVERSE. AVERSE is the verb meaning oppose (you are AVERSE to it). ADVERSE is the adjective meaning bad (ADVERSE weather).
10. BESIDES, BESIDE. BESIDE means at the side of, and BESIDES means in addition to.
11. BLOCK, BLOC. BLOC is a coalition or group with the same goal.
12. COMPOSE, COMPRISE. You COMPOSE things by putting them together Once they are together, the object COMPRISES or includes various parts.
13. CONSENSUS. CONSENSUS means general agreement. Therefore, it is redundant to say CONSENSUS of opinion.
14. COUNCIL, COUNSEL. COUNCIL means an assembly while COUNSEL means to give advice.
15. COUPLE OF. You need the OF. Don't say "in a couple minutes."
16. DEMOLISH, DESTROY. They mean to do away with completely. There is no such meaning as partially DESTROYED or no need to say totally DEMOLISH.
17. DIE OF. One DIES OF an illness not from it. Also, a person DIES after an operation, not from or as a result of, or following, an operation.
18. DIFFERENT FROM. Things are DIFFERENT FROM each other, not different than.
19. DROWN. Don't say someone was DROWNED unless the victim's head was held under. Say: John Jones DROWNED last night, not John Jones was DROWNED.
20. DUE TO, OWING TO, BECAUSE OF. The past phrase is preferable.
21. ECOLOGY, ENVIRONMENT. ECOLOGY is the study of the relationship between organisms and ENVIRONMENT.
22. EITHER. It means one or the other, not both.
23. FARTHER, FURTHER. FARTHER applies to distance, and FURTHER means in addition to.
24. FLIERS, FLYERS. Airmen and handbills are fliers.
25. FLOUT, FLAUNT. FLOUT means to mock or to show disdain. FLAUNT means to display showingly.
26. FUNERAL SERVICE. A funeral is a service. Leave out service.
27. HEAD UP. Leave off the up. People HEAD committees; they do not HEAD UP committees. People make rules, they don't make them up. People take skiing lessons, etc.
28. HEALTHFUL, HEALTHY. HEALTHFUL means to cause health, while HEALTHY means possessing health.
29. IMPLY, INFER. The speaker IMPLIES while the hearer INFERS.
30. IN ADVANCE OF, PRIOR TO, BEFORE. Use BEFORE; it's more natural.
31. IT'S, ITS. IT'S is the contraction for it is. ITS is the possessive pronoun.
32. LEAVE, LET. LEAVE alone means depart from or to isolate. LET means to permit or allow.

33. LESS, FEWER. LESS applies to situations using the singular form, while FEWER applies to the plural. "They have FEWER members now, and the chairman has LESS income."
34. LIKE, AS. In general use LIKE to compare pronouns; use AS when comparing phrases or clauses containing a verb. However, like is increasingly being used as a substitute for as or as if in informal usage.
35. MARSHALL, MARSHAL. MARSHALL is correct only on a proper name. Otherwise, use MARSHAL for verb or noun.
36. MEAN, AVERAGE, MEDIAN. Use AVERAGE for the sum of components divided by number of components. MEAN designates a figure between two extremes. MEDIAN is the number that has as many numbers above it as below it.
37. MEDIA, DATA, ALUMNI. Plural forms of medium, datum, and alumnus.
38. OPINION, ESTIMATION. OPINION is a judgment, and ESTIMATION is an evaluation or guess.
39. ORAL, VERBAL. Use ORAL when use of the mouth is involved and VERBAL when writing is used, although it may apply to both spoken or written words.
40. OVER, MORE THAN. OVER refers to the spatial relationships, while MORE THAN is used with figures.
41. PEDDLE, PEDAL. PEDDLE refers to selling, while PEDAL refers to some form of locomotion.
42. PRINCIPAL, PRINCIPLE. A rule of truth is a PRINCIPLE, while the first or dominant thing is the PRINCIPAL one.
43. RELUCTANT, RETICENT. If a person doesn't want to act, he is RELUCTANT. If he doesn't want to speak, he is RETICENT.
44. SINCE, BECAUSE. SINCE is time-related, while BECAUSE is action-related.
45. THAT, WHICH. THAT tends to restrict the reader's thought and direct it in the way you want it to go. WHICH is non-sensitive and gives subsidiary information.
46. UNDER WAY, NOT UNDERWAY. But don't say someting got UNDER WAY unless it's a ship. Say it began or started.
47. UNIQUE. Something that is UNIQUE is one of its kind. It can't be very, quite, rather, or somewhat UNIQUE.
48. UP. Don't use it as a verb.
49. USE ALL RIGHT, NOT ALRIGHT.
50. WHO'S, WHOSE. WHO'S is a contraction for who is. WHOSE is possessive.

GRAMMAR

While a detailed knowledge of grammar is helpful to the copy editor, a working knowledge of the major grammatical principles is essential. The following list of 10 basic grammatical rules should provide a review for you as a beginning copy editor.

RULE NO. 1   *Verbs must agree with their subjects in number and persons.*

          Example: We are; you are; he is.

RULE NO. 2 *Words intervening between the subject and verb do not affect the number of the verb.*

> **Example:** *Improvements* in the Visual Display Terminal *have* not increased the cost.

RULE NO. 3 *When the subject is one of the following words, the verb must be singular; anybody, each, every, everybody, nobody and either. Neither and none usually require a singular verb.*

> **Example:** Each of the reporters has filed a story.
> Neither of the editors is going.

However, if neither is used to link plural nouns, a plural verb is used.

> **Example:** Neither reporters nor editors have come to the university for three years.

RULE NO. 4 *When the subject is a collective noun, consider the subject singular or plural depending on the meaning you wish to convey. If the meaning of the subject is a collective body, use the singular; however, if you are thinking of individuals within the collective body, use the plural.*

> **Example:** The newspaper staff is planning a special edition.
>
> The newspaper staff are listed individually by position on page 2 of today's paper.

RULE NO. 5 *Verb tenses should indicate the correct sequence of action; therefore, a verb in a subordinate clause should be consistent with the verb tense in the main clause.*

> **Example:** When the makeup editor finished the page, she realized she had made a mistake.

RULE NO. 6 *Use active voice for most verbs. Passive voice may be used to emphasize the receiver of an action (such as the injured in a car accident), or to emphasize an indefinite statement.*

> **Example:** Write, "The boy hit the ball," rather than, "The ball was hit by the boy."
>
> However, to emphasize the receiver of the action, you may write, "The woman was injured in the auto crash."

RULE NO. 7 *Modifiers must be located closely enough to the word or phrases they modify for the reader to be able to distinguish clearly what they modify.*

> **Incorrect Example:** Referring to your memo yesterday, the change is being made. (Dangling modifier).
>
> **Correct Example:** Referring to your memo yesterday, the editors are changing the situations.

To correct dangling modifiers, either change from passive to active voice in order to have the participle modify the doer of the action, or change the participle to a clause.

RULE NO. 8 *Make the elements in a series grammatically parallel. Adjectives should be linked with other adjectives, adverbs with adverbs, infinitives with infinitives, and so forth.*

    Incorrect Example: The TV station manager plans to install new videotape equipment, to hire three new employees, and build a new news set.

    Correct Example: The TV station manager plans to install new videotape equipment, to hire three new employees and to build a new news set.

In the correct example all three of the manager's plans were put in the infinitive form.

RULE NO. 9 *Pronouns must clearly refer to their antecedents.*

    Incorrect Example: The editor told the young reporter that his statement was incorrect. (Whose statement does his refer to?)

    Correct Example: The editor said that the young reporter's statement was incorrect.

RULE NO. 10 *The case of a pronoun must suit the function of the pronoun.*

    (1) *Pronouns used as an object of a preposition must take the objective case.*

        Example: He came with me.

    (2) *A pronoun used as an appositive must agree with the word it explains.*

        Example: Only two reporters, John and I, could go to the speech. (I refers to the subject; therefore, the pronoun must be in the subjective case.)

    (3) *A pronoun modifying the gerund must take the possessive case.*

        Example: The audience appreciated your lecturing them without fear.

Name_____   **Exercise 12**

Directions: Turn these into acceptable, concise sentences.

1. Tom tipped the scales at 260 pounds.
2. In conjunction with the new policy, the company now requires payment at the end of the month.
3. He was killed when he came into contact with a live electrical wire.
4. The man was found in a dying condition at the side of the road.
5. The four men entered a plea of guilty.
6. He placed the letter in the mails.
7. She lifted up her glass.
8. He arrived at his conclusion that the chemical was dangerous yesterday.
9. The new recruit arrived at the base.
10. The meeting was brought to a close at 10:30 p.m. that night.
11. They will make their home in Loveland.
12. The end of the present month will bring to a close the series of games.
13. Brisk business is expected this weekend because of the fact that Monday is a holiday.
14. Coroner Dr. Sam G. Smith paid a visit to the new lab.
15. The regular monthly luncheon meeting will be held tomorrow.
16. Sally Moore will give vocal selections according to an announcement made today by the chairman of the program.
17. She made a long distance telephone call to Los Angeles from Baltimore.
18. The man dropped out of sight.
19. Henry Aiken sustained a broken right ankle.
20. The chairman admitted that he was in receipt of the communication from the board.
21. He went to Austin for the purpose of interviewing the new governor of Texas.
22. The senator made clear his opposition to the land use bill during the course of the interview.

Name_____ **Exercise 13**

Directions: Edit these into acceptable, concise sentences.

1. K. Roger Wynn, former mayor of Central Valley who resides at 218 City Circle, died today of a heart attack in the study of his Central Valley home. He was 62 years old.

    Wynn was considered a possibility as a vice-president nominee for the Republican party in 1968. Had he been nominated by the Republicans at that time he would have been the first politician to Jewish national ever so honored by a major political party.

    ###

2. The men, both of Central Valley were arrested yesterday afternoon at 2:45 p.m. for stealing 200 dollars from the house of Mr. and Mrs. Floyd Mathis, whose home is at 27 Woodland Avenue.

    ###

3. An agreement has been made to buy Getty Oil Company by Texaco, Inc., one of America's largest oil manufacturers. Nearly $10 billion will finalize what will be the largest corporate marriage in U.S. history. The court delaying the deal had been lifted.

    ###

4. Ross E. Wright, Central Valley University has taken a position as librarian at a Mississippi college. Wright is to become librarian of Etta Vena, Miss., on January 21. Wright served as archivest at Central U. for the past 17 years after graduating from Ohio University with a degree of library science.

    ###

Name_____ **Exercise 14**

GRAMMAR EXERCISE

Directions: Edit the following sentences to conform with Associated Press style. Correct all errors, including typographical and spelling.

1. Clear presentation and simple style makes this a style book you will want for your classroom.

2. The Middle East increases intensity everyday, peace-keeping forces seem to aggravate peace rather than promoting it.

3. When the letter you want to the Business Office was not forwarded, there was naturally some confusion between their accounting division and I.

4. Neither of these possibilities were explained in your query to us.

5. We were pleased to learn that the crowd at your tour were so enthusiastic about the new presses.

6. If anyone else was in his beat, they would do the same thing.

7. The editor who had sent three orders and two requests for engraving machines were visited by our representative.

8. Beginning work on his survey on a Monday, he found he was not paid, until the following week.

9. The reported of the story and not the three accountants who supplied the facts and cost estimates believe the charge is necessary.

10. This crusade was conducted to reduce the number of fatal highway accidents at the end of the year which was successful.

11. By eating less food, weight should be lost by John.

12. Employing such communication media as newspapers, radio and television, the campaign platform of the party was presented.

13. I don't believe anyone besides the editor checks the copy as carefully as himself.

14. The newsroom staff were planning to attend the local Community Chest Luncheon at which the results of our newspaper's giving was to be announced.

15. Your approval as well as those of two members of your Board of Directors are required to approve the survey.
16. Included in the group invited to attend the broadcasters conference were three anchormen — Mr. Akers, you, and me.
17. The Annual Report together with our last two quarterly reports to shareholders are being sent sent to you by our Business Office.
18. The new restaurant operates continuous, around the clock, twenty-four hours a day.
19. A person like you who pays their subscription promptly is the backbone of American magazines.
20. The publishers disagreed and has to meet again.
21. Referring to our telephone interview yesterday, the information you requested for are enclosed.
22. Concluding that this press was a poor risk, the question was submitted to the business office for decision.
23. To accommodate more employees, we are recieving less time for breaks from the company.
24. Will you please let us know who sent you the original tip to since it apparently was not received at the newsroom.
25. Everybody in our radio station want to express their appreciation to you for your thoughtfulness.

Name_____   **Exercise 15**

Directions: Edit the story.

DRUG LAB

The Collins Health Department in cooperation with Central Valley University has opened a new drug analysis laboratory to help aid the students and faculty of CVU and the residents of the greater Central Valley area said McDonald. The laboratory is for the analysis of anonymous drug samples only.

To prevent local dealers from using this service as a quality control lab, the CHD Drug Information Team will only report the drug or drugs presented in the sample submitted. The technique they use, to analyze drugs, Thin Layer Chromatography, allows the team to report and detect dangerous quantities present in samples submitted for testing.

The laboratory is open to every student and faculty member of CVU, and every resident of Central Valley, and is free of charge.

According to Marlene McDonald, supervisor of the program, this service is a use useful and beneficial one because, firstly if a person wants to take a drug, he/seh can find out the content of what he/she is taking, rather than relyingon word-of-mouth. Secondly, if a drug is cut with harmful adulterants, a report to the person may prevent harmful injury. Also, if the drug has been cut with harmful adulterants, this report may prevent serious injury. By keeping a record of current drugs in this area, the drug team, Marlene pointed out that the drugk team will be able to assist the hospitals in emergency room treatment of overdoses.

To protect those using this service, they are required to follow procedures prescribed by law exactly.

Official forms which most accompany drug samples may be acquired at the activities desk in the student center at Central Valley University, at the State Health center, and the at the Drug information Team's office in the basebment of the Second National Bank Building.

###

Name_____ **Exercise 16**

Directions: Edit the story.

JACKSON

General George Jackson, retired Marine general of the United States, will not be speaking to teh Central Valley University student body as scheduled. His sudden concellation was told to a Central Valley Free Press reporter today by Jerry Walker, a sophmore from Tampa, Florida. Jerry is secretary of the campus chapter of the Society and organizer, promoter, and coordinator for the Fall Convocation.

The retired military general was to address the students of the Central Valley student body on the topic of "What has ahppened to the Bright Students on College Campuses?" A new speaker has been announced to the generals place on the program. Jeff A Kimbell, a former student at Central Valley and a former Republican official, will speak on "How Our Campuses Have Been Subverted." This promises to be an interesting topic, according to Walker.

Jeff Kimball has been with the Society for a Responsible Campus since it was formed six years ago. He is a former student of Central Valley University and Central Valley High School. Since General George B. Jackson was called away personal reasons, mainly health, Jeff offered to fly in and speak.

Jerry Walker said that all other planned and scheduled activities are to be held as announced previously. "The Central Valley University chapter of the Society for a Responsible Campus is expecting a high turnout to concerned students about the responsible campus life, responsible citizenship, responsible education, and responsible government," he added.

###

Name _____   **Exercise 17**

Directions: Edit the story.

DOG ORDINANCE

The ordnance regulating dogs was adopted by the city council last night, ending a year's discussion of the subject.

Provisions of the law spell out when a dog must be on a leash or confined to the property of the owner. There is no time a dog is permitted to run loose outside the owner's property.

If a dog is picked up by the city dog warden, the dog is impounded. To reclaim a dog, the owner must pay a $10 fee for impounding and $1.00 a day. He also must post a $50.00 bond until proof of vaccination is shown for the dog. The fine for the second offense by a dog owner is $25.00.

The city council offered the argument that sufficient public complaint had been expressed about dogs running loose to arrive at the conclusion that the city needed a law with teeth in it.

###

Chapter 4

Writing Headlines

Headlines serve four major purposes. They attract attention, quickly inform the reader what the story is about, grade or evaluate the story by type size and column width of the headline, and help establish the overall tone of the publication.

Before considering the forms or content of headlines, two unfamiliar units of measurement must be mastered — the point and the pica.

The point is the smaller of the two and serves as the basis for the printer's measuring system. One point is equal to 1/72 of an inch; one inch, therefore, is equal to 72 points.

Points are used most commonly to express vertical dimensions, particularly the size of the type and the amount of leading (white space between consecutive lines of type). Point size is the distance from the top of an ascender to the bottom of a descender, NOT the size of any one letter.

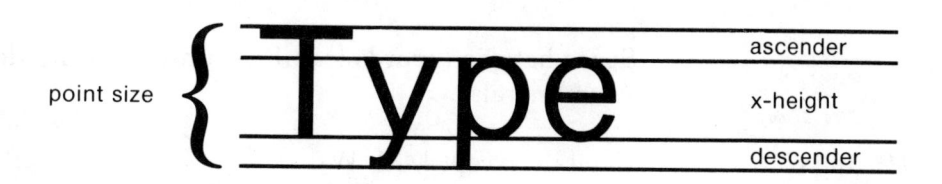

Type comes in standard sizes. Body type sizes range from 5-point to 12-point, including 5½, 6, 6½, 7, 8, 9, 10, and 11. Display, or headline, type begins at 14-point and increases in size by larger increments: 14, 18, 24, 30, 36, 42, 48, 54, 60, 72, 84, 96, etc.

The pica is the larger of the printer's measuring units. One pica is equal to 12 points or 1/6 of an inch; 6 picas, therefore, is equal to 1 inch.

Picas are most commonly used to express horizontal dimensions, particularly the width of a line or column of type and the width of the gutters (white space between columns of type). A column 12 picas wide is 2 inches or 144 points wide; an 18-pica column is 3 inches or 216 points wide; and so on.

Each line of a headline must be made to fit the width allotted to it. Unlike the spacing method on a standard typewriter, type is set using proportional spacing — that is, each letter is allocated space according to its width. Because typesetting recognizes that some letters (l, for instance) are thinner than others (m, for instance), simply counting letters is not an accurate method for fitting type, particularly the large type used in headlines.

Consider the difference between "Illegal" and "Mammon." If the editor were to count letters, he would conclude that "Illegal" (7 letters) is a longer word than "Mammon" (6 letters). But look at what happens when those words are set in type:

Illegal
Mammon

"Mammon," because it has three extra-wide letters, is much longer than "Illegal," which has four extra-narrow letters.

Headline writers solve this problem of proportional spacing by counting not the letters, but the unit values assigned to the letters on the basis of whether they are narrower or wider than an average letter. The average letters are assigned a value of 1 unit; narrower letters are counted as ½ unit, wider letters as 1½ or 2. The unit counts used for cap- and lowercase headlines are below:

1/2 unit:	Lower case l, i, f, t
	Punctuation . , ' : ; ( ) ! -
1 unit:	Most lower case letters and Capital I
	Punctuation ? $ % ¢ " & ®
	Space between words (can be counted ½ if needed)
	All numerals
1½ units:	Capitals except I, M, W
	Lower case m and w
	Punctuation — (em dash)
2 units:	Capitals M and W

Headlines usually are assigned by a selected number scheme such as 3-36-2. The first number means the number of columns, the second one is the type size, and the last number means the number of lines in the headline. A 3-36-2 would be a 3-column, 36-point, 2-line headline.

Most publications have a headline schedule that shows allowable headline forms and the maximum unit counts for each line. The minimum unit count for a headline is a matter of editor preference, but commonly 2 units less than the maximum. No headline should extend less than half-way across the last column of the body type with which it goes. See Appendix B for the Central Valley Free Press headline schedule.

Notice that the headline schedule shows the maximum count for a full column-width headline. If the headline and story are to be set in a box, both the pica width of the body type and the headline count will have to be shortened. Boxing a story usually shortens a headline by about 2 units.

While there are many formats for headlines, the flush-left style is considered the most functional because it provides the reader with a consistent axis of orientation. (See Graphics chapter)

a. **Flush Left**

Collegian Newspaper
Wins Pulitzer Prize

Some of the other popular formats include:

b. **Centered**

Collegian Newspaper
Wins Pulitzer Prize

c. **Hanging Indention**

Waco City Council
Hears Judge Honda
Attack Water Plan

d. **Pyramid**

Gov. Andrews
Condemns Newsweek
For 'Bias' in Student Riots

e. **Inverted Pyramid**

Gov. Andrews Condemns Newsweek
For 'News Bias'
In Riots

f. **Drop-line**

Gov. Andrews Condemns
Newsweek for 'Bias'
In CU Student Riots

HEADLINE FORMS

Headlines often take one of four forms. The most common is the headline by itself. It may have a kicker, a deck or a box.

A kicker is a headline above the main head set off with a short rule. It normally is used for feature stories when the headline writer can be more creative. Often italicized, the kicker is set in approximately one half the type size of the main headline.

a. **Kicker**

5 Dead
Police Seek Mystery Killer

A deck is one headline under another with the second headline usually telling the second most important element of the story. If the first headline is set in more columns than the second, then the second one also would be called a "readout."

b. **Deck**

BELEW ASSAILS CHARGES OF BRIBERY
Dixon Trust
Unaffected,
Press Told

A headline set in a box (story and headline enclosed in line rules) should be about two counts less than the maximum allowed in the headline schedule.

c. **Box**

ROBBS MOVE TO NEW HOME

Richmond, Va. — The Charles S. Robbs have moved into their new home, a three-story Georgian brick structure.

Robb was . . . .

One of the arguments among copy editors concerns the rules for writing a headline. Wide differences exist in standards and practices among newspapers throughout the country. For instance, most newspapers avoid using "and" in a heading; yet, there are some well-known papers that use "and" regularly.

The following suggestions for headline writing, then, are presented as just that — suggested guidelines. They will not be mastered in one reading, but it will take much practice to become a skilled headline writer. Many of the following chapters in this workbook include headline assignments.

SUGGESTED GUIDELINES FOR HEADLINE WRITING

1. Use subjects, verbs, and objects in headlines; they are shortened sentences.
2. Use verbs in active voice unless the object is the most important element (e.g., car accident).
3. Avoid forms of the verb "to be" or "to have."
4. Omit the articles "a," "an" and "the."
5. Use a comma to substitute for "and."
6. Divide different ideas by a semicolon; never use a period.
7. Use present or future tense for verbs.
8. Use single rather than double quotation marks.
9. Never split words between lines. Avoid splitting verbal, prepositional and other phrases between lines.
10. Use precise numerals (except "one" when it begins the headline).
11. Do not editorialize.
12. Avoid using names except when they are readily identifiable or for obituaries.
13. Use the same style and spelling as the story.
14. Avoid negative or tentative (may) headlines.
15. Be specific, concise. Avoid generalities.

Name_____   **Exercise 18**

HEADLINE WRITING EXERCISE

Directions: This exercise is designed to introduce you to the skills and problems of headline writing. Answer the following questions.

1. **The headline writer must be able to use synonyms for words and phrases. Often a word or phrase will not fit into a headline and must be condensed. The headline writer must remember, though, to be accurate and fair.**

   Write four synonyms that have fewer letters for "substantiate."

   _____   _____

   _____   _____

   One word can often be used instead of a phrase. Shorten the following phrases:

   Due to the fact   ____Because,_____ (example)

   At this time   _____

   Attain success   _____

   Side of the road   _____

   During the time   _____

2. **Good headlines have active verbs in present tense.**

   Weak: Prices Will Be Greatly Higher
   Stronger: Prices To Rise Sharply

   Weak: Baltimore Wins Football Game Over Los Angeles
   Stronger: Colts Whip Rams

   Try to improve these heads:

   President's Moscow Trip Set for June 10

   _____

   Cuban Revolt Seen by Secretary of State

   _____

3. **Each headline should tell the most important element first.**

   Wrong:
       At Central Valley
       3 Die in Fire

   Correct:
       3 Die in Fire
       At Central Valley

   Revise these headlines by putting the most important thing first:

   Anonymous Donor Gives   _____

   $5000 to CVU Student   _____

   Administration Receives   _____

   13 Demands from CVU Radicals   _____

4. **Try a headline for yourself. Make it two lines for a Central Valley newspaper; don't worry about length at this point. Here's the story:**

   PORTLAND, Ore. — A Portland couple and three boys they were babysitting were murdered late Monday evening.

   The victims were identified as George A. Green, 31; his wife, Arlene, 30; Tom Anderson, 8; Andy Anderson, 6; and Richard Anderson, 2.

   Officials said the murders probably occurred Monday evening about 8. One officer called the slaying "the most violent crime I have ever seen in many years of police work."

   Write your headline here.

   _____

   _____

5. **Headlines should be divided at the most appropriate spot.**

   Try not to break up compound verbs.
       Treasury Secretary Tries to
       Halt U.S. Gold, Silver Outflow

Avoid splitting prepositional and adjectival phrases.

> Laborers Want Hike in
> Wage, Fringe Demands

The verb goes at the end of the first line when possible.

> New York Shivers
> Under 10-inch Snow

Change the following heads by avoiding awkward splits. You also may substitute words, but keep the same number of lines.

Congressman Will _____

Resign Tomorrow _____

Senate May _____

Consider New _____

Drug Bill Today _____

6. **Headlines should not go farther than the story. Avoid editorializing in a headline or your headline will load a story with unwarranted meaning. Verbs of attribution such as "admits," "denies," "asserts," "accuses," and "points out," are biased per se, and should not be used. Eliminate the editorializing from these heads:**

James Cey, Kidnapper _____

Goes On Trial Monday _____

In District Court _____

Cops Nab 40 Crooks _____

In Gambling Raid _____

Trustees Hit Students

With Stiff Tuition

7. Punctuate headlines sparingly.

Periods are used only in abbreviations.

A comma replaces "and," but not any other part of speech.

The semi-colon replaces an internal period.

Single quotes are used in place of double quotes.

Correct this headline.

40% in east, and South, Think

President is Doing "Good Job."

8. On many small and medium-sized newspapers headlines are capitalized as though they were regular sentences. This is called "modified downstyle." Some larger newspapers still use "modified upstyle" headlines. The latter are capitalized like book titles.
   In modified upstyle every word in a headline is capitalized except prepositions, articles, and conjunctions, However, even these are capped if they begin a line.

Modified Downstyle	Modified Upstyle
Rams win over UCLA	Rams Win Over UCLA

Capitalize this headline correctly according to modified downstyle:

pay cuts for students
by trustees to cause 'revolt'

Capitalize the above headline
now using modified upstyle:

9. **Use subjects, verbs, and objects in headlines. Use verbs in active voice except in rare cases where the object is the most important element. Headlines that have no verbs are called "label heads."**

   Rewrite the following "label heads"

   Study of President's tax			_____
   records by Congress
   						_____

   Pianist, artist winners			_____
   of Young Artist award
   						_____

10. **Headlines must fit in the available space.**

    Headline counting is part of the typographic translation. Each editor must be sure that his words will fit into a given space.
    If the copy editor writes a headline that's too long for the space, the printer will leave off a word or send back the head and swear a great deal. In "cold type" printing, however, there is less need for concern if the headline doesn't fit. Changes are easier even though the swearing may be the same!
    In type, different letters have different widths; consequently, the editor cannot simply count each letter as "one." However, most lower case letters are given a 1 count. Check the introductory material of this chapter for the various "counts." Count the following headline:

    21 Dancers Fired; 'Won't Undress'   Total = _____

    You should count the spaces between the words and the total should be 32½. If you don't get that total, try it again.

    A headline schedule is a listing of commonly used headline sizes of a newspaper. The editor and the printer each have a copy. The schedule indicates the type size, the number of lines, and the count per line. See Appendix B for the full headline schedule for the Central Valley Free Press.

    2-24-2 (18-20) is a typical designation for a head.

    "2" means the width, in columns, of the headline.
    "24" means it is set in 24-point type of a given type face.
    The second "2" means it has two lines.
    "(18-20)" means that the minimum count is 18, and the maximum is 20.
    Such a head, with its designation, might look like this:

    2-24-2 (18-20)   *Count the headline:*

    CVU students protest   *The first line is* _____ *counts.*
    campus book prices
                                    The second line is _____ *counts.*

Here's a headline and its designation. Does it fit?

3-36-2 (13-15)

President summons   Count _____
special session
                           Count _____

If it doesn't fit, rewrite it below. Save time by changing as little as possible.

_____

_____

Write a headline for the following stories.

4-36-2 (22-24)

_____ (Count _____)

_____ (Count _____)

    Thomas J. Glenn, president of the First National Bank of Central Valley, was named Wednesday to the board of trustees of Collins County Memorial Hospital.
    Glenn, 36, was appointed to finish three years of the five-year term of Mary Eddy, who moved to Austin last month.

2-30-2 (16-18)

_____ (Count _____)

_____ (Count _____)

    The major land use bill of the current legislative session goes through the lawmakers' wringer again Wednesday.
    The bill would require local governments to protect various areas and activities of state interest from rampant development.
    Sen. Dan R. Mills, R-Central Valley, said that the chance for early passage seems dim.

Name_____   **Exercise 19**

HEADLINE WRITING PRACTICE

Directions: This exercise is designed to give you more practice in writing headlines. Use the headline schedule in Appendix B for the headline count. Write the heads within two counts of the maximum, but in no case should you exceed the maximum.

1. Write a 2-24-2 headline for the following story. Use 8-column format.

   ATHENS, Ga. — An intense search for the mass killers of a farm family of six spread across the South Wednesday and officials expressed fear they could strike "again and again."
   A seventh victim already may have been left behind in Pennsylvania.
   The chief suspects in the case are three men who broke out of a work camp May 5 in Wicomico County, Md. They were identified as Wayne Carl Seaman, 26, serving 10 years for robbery; Carl Doyle, 19, serving four years for burglary, and George Knowles, 35, serving 18 months for contempt of court. William Newport, Doyle, 15, William's brother, reportedly was traveling with them.
   They are sought here in the slaying of Ned Richter, 62, his brother, Aubrey, 56, his sons, Jerry, 35, James, 25, Chester, 32, and Jerry's wife, Mary, 24. The bodies of the five men were discovered Tuesday in a mobile home on a large farm the Richter's run. Mary's nude body was found about six miles from the trailer. She had been sexually molested.
   The killers, believed to be heavily-armed, apparently made their getaway in a car belonging to Jerry Richter and bearing Georgia license plate number MIY 634.

   ###

   _____ COUNT _____
   _____ COUNT _____

2. Write a 3-48-2 head for the above story using 6-column format.

   _____ COUNT _____
   _____ COUNT _____

3. Write a 2-24-1 head for the same story using 6-column format.

   _____ COUNT _____
   _____ COUNT _____
   _____ COUNT _____

4. Write a 4-48-1 headline for the following news story using 6-column format.

　　AUSTIN, Tex. — A virtual ban on fireworks was approved by the Texas Senate Tuesday despite warnings from opponents the legislation was an "effort in futility" and one of the "most gross errors" the Senate ever made.

　　The Senate on a 24-8 vote approved the fireworks ban and sent the bill to the House for approval.

　　The proposed law bans all private use and sale of fireworks with the exception of sparklers and caps. Community-approved fireworks displays also would be legal. The measure would go into effect in about a year.

　　Sens. Ted Locust, R-Waco, and George Johnson, R-Texas City, expressed most of the opposition to the bill prior to its winning approval on final reading.

　　"I think the action taken by this body . . . is one of the most gross errors this body could have ever made," said Locust, president pro tem of the Senate. "This type of action on our part is going to come back and haunt everybody."

　　Johnson said he knew of five states which had tried a total ban on fireworks, only to come back later and rescind the action.

###

_____ COUNT _____

5. Write a 2-18-3 headline for the previous story using 6-column format.

_____ COUNT _____

_____ COUNT _____

_____ COUNT _____

6. Write a 3-24-1 headline for the following story using 5-column tabloid format.

　　Those of you who have only two weeks left to do that term paper that counts for half your grade will be relieved to hear that the library staff has volunteered its free time just to help you late starters.

　　Library representatives Tim Napoleon and Sandra Alexander announced that for the next two weekends (the 12th and 13th and the 19th and 20th) extra personnel will be available to help students with their research.

　　From one o'clock to five o'clock on Saturdays and from two o'clock to six o'clock on Sundays, the extra staff will be available to answer questions and help locate needed materials.

　　In particular, people will be available in the Microtext Rooms, the catalog area, the periodical area, the science reference desk, and the document collection. Additional people will be shelving and ready to help anyone with locating a book on the shelves.

###

_____ COUNT _____

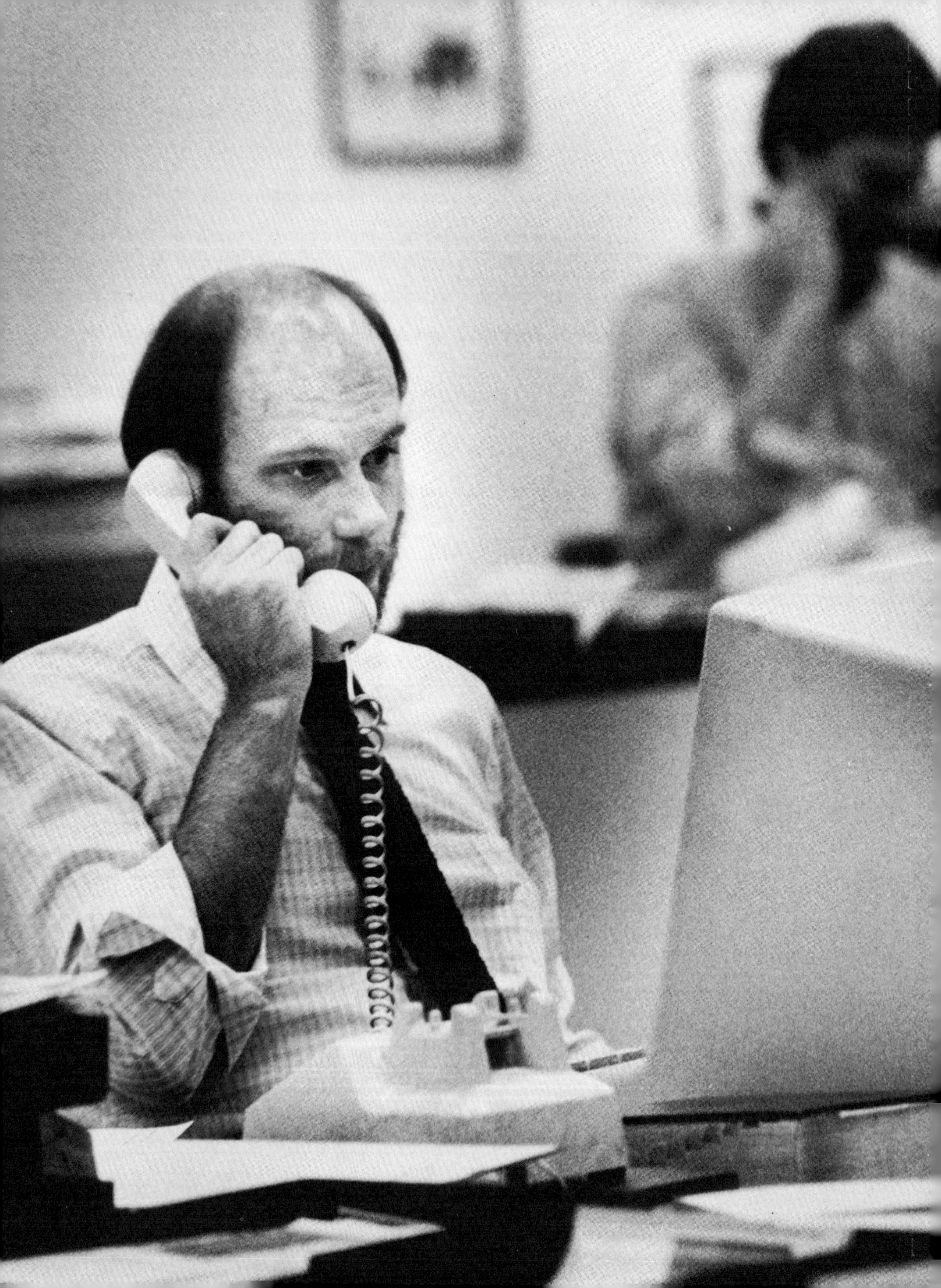

Chapter 5
Selecting News

News definitions vary among editors and textbooks because news can include almost any event or opinion. As a result, selection of news items tend to differ from medium to medium, but the types of news used by a particular medium are somewhat constant, i.e., a poultry magazine tends to use stories on chickens and ducks.

In the news selection process much depends on how an editor and reporter view news sources, events and the news audience. Events of national and international scope often have a higher selection rate by a metropolitan newspaper editor than by one editing news in a much smaller population center. The metropolitan news editor may feel the audience needs to know more about national and international events and is more interested in them. A news editor in a smaller community may choose stories of regional importance, and then he or she will use national and international items when they may be especially important to the local audience.

"The news," David Brinkley of ABC News once said, "is what I say it is." Brinkley and thousands of other journalists around the country decide each day for millions what is news and what is not. The process of news selection involves countless judgments. Most people never read the paper from front to back; they *select* what to read based on their interests of the moment.

When you read the paper a headline may catch your eye and lure you into the story. A picture on the sports page might do the same thing. If the story doesn't capture and hold you, you can bail out and move to the next story. You can choose in what order you read the newspaper — comics first, back to front, sports, then editorials, or perhaps only the crossword puzzle.

Another facet of news judgment by editors depends upon the amount of space allotted for news stories, the number of wire and syndicated items available and the number of news reporters working for that medium. News reaches the newspaper through various sources. It is assembled by editors. Information from all over the world is relayed from the Associated Press and United Press International. Wire services, machines, two-way radios, telephones and police monitors blare in the newsroom throughout the day, alerting the city editor to breaking news within the community.

All this information would, if published in its entirety, fill many times the day's news hole. Instead it must be processed and distilled into compact reports that will give the most important and interesting events of the day. With so much news and so little space to tell it, audiences would do well to use several media for their news.

NEWS JUDGMENT

The judgments involved in the news process are as individual as the people who make them. How do you decide what makes the biggest story of the day? What other stories should be included? How long should they be? Even the networks don't always agree on the lead story of the day. Experience is the best teacher in answering such questions, but you can follow guidelines of common sense as you select the stories you will use.

News judgment requires the same discipline as any other skill, and you must develop it over time. Begin to study newspapers you respect. Study their news judgment, talk with news personnel about what makes news, and practice making news judgments in your everyday life. Learn to distinguish what is serious and significant, what events are essential to know about, what stories affect your life directly, which stories are nice to know about but have little impact in your life, which stories exist by themselves and which are "manufactured," i.e., wouldn't exist if you didn't cover them.

Besides these factors, news judgment includes a variety of news elements such as proximity and timeliness of an event. Other news elements include novelty, prominence, human interest, suspense, and conflict. The news lead of a story should include the most important element of news available. While there is no standard formula for news selection, all the following factors and elements are interrelated and play a part in the news selection process.

Timeliness

News is what happens now, what happens in the immediate present or what will happen. The straight news story must deal with recent or future events. Yesterday's news is old news and isn't reported unless there is a new development. Timeliness is much less important in feature news.

Proximity

News is what happens close to us, either emotionally or geographically. We tend to be interested in events that happen within our community because quite often they interest or affect us in some way. Who can hear of a car-train collision without wondering for a split second whether the victim is someone we might know? Who, in a community, is not affected by rising property values or increased taxes? Who is not interested in some way about the drought or the approaching storm?

We also have tremendous affinity for reports of interesting events that happen far away from us. Sometimes, if the event is big enough, it far overshadows the less important happenings in our own community. Examples include war and disaster stories, the moon landings or the discovery of Stone Age tribes living on a South Sea island.

Whether you are dealing with local, national or world news, learn to "read" it as your audience would; determine what is most momentous, most interesting or most significant about the story you are writing.

Significance

News is what is significant to your audience. Whatever the story, ask yourself who is affected by it, or is interested in it. In a metropolitan area, a story about a teacher's strike, while important, may directly affect only about one of every 20 people in your audience, while a story about dramatic increases in food prices or a developing cold front may affect almost everyone listening. Always ask yourself, as you assess the potential significance of the story, how it affects your audience.

Conflict

News is what results in dramatic conflict and hence human interest. Dramatic conflict is whatever happens between two opposing forces. The conflict can be between one person and another or one nation and another or it can be between man and an outside influence or force. In simplified form, dramatic conflict occurs in four basic definitions:

- *man versus man*

    The struggle between individuals in a boxing match, a chess championship, or a senator's fight against organized labor; other examples include the test pilot who fights to keep his job after mandatory retirement age, clashes between pro and anti-abortion forces, the women's rights movement, or the story of an elderly woman on welfare struggling to avoid eviction from her home.

- *man versus himself*

    The struggle of a person to kick drug addiction; the triumph of athletic achievement in a single-person sport; the triumph of an individual over a physical handicap.

- *man versus fate*

    The struggle of an individual to survive after a wilderness plane crash until help arrives; a public figure's fight against cancer; shipwrecks; families made homeless by fires and disasters.

- *man versus nature*

    Significant weather events; consequences of air and water pollution; environmental health stories; stories of individuals who cross the sea alone, by balloon, or by sailboat.

Prominence

News is what happens to prominent people, places or things. Nearly everyone is interested in the prominent names that make news. Everyone from the president and his family to pop singers and motorcycle daredevils attract our attention. Often such newsmakers provide us with vicarious experiences in the activities and achievements in which we would participate in real life if only we had the chance, the courage or the ability. Go to a bar or a dorm lounge and try watching people listen to radio or television news. You will discover that prominent names in the news capture and recapture their attention during the course of a newscast. Similarly, the famous places and things in our lives — from the Washington Monument to our favorite city landmark — perk our interest in the news.

Human Interest

Human Interest. Ultimately, news is anything people are interested in, whether significant or trivial. If you think a story would interest a majority of your audience, it is probably newsworthy.

An understanding of news helps you highlight the elements you should search for in each story you write; it helps you define treatment and style for any story because it offers a way of extracting the essence of any event for emphasis in your lead. Let's look at an example.

Firemen are going on strike for higher pay at 6 a.m. tomorrow if wage negotiations aren't ironed out by that time. They want an average wage increase of 70 cents an hour, or a total additional cost for fire protection services of about $1.5 million. The property tax increase needed to cover the higher wages would amount to an average of $6 per household in the community. City and fire union representatives are meeting late into the night.

This story contains all elements that fall within the definition of news. The story is happening now; it is happening close to us; it has the potential to affect us financially, emotionally and perhaps even physically if the community is left without fire protection should the strike materialize. Dramatic conflict is present in the form of man versus man —firemen are taking drastic action to force a response from the city — and prominent community leaders are helping resolve the problem.

In your selection of news for the Central Valley area, you need to make your news decisions based on all the news elements and factors, but especially on proximity and timeliness of the event. You are editing news for an audience in a community of about 50,000, and when possible, wire or bureau stories should be localized. The news element of proximity may be reflected particularly in the lead and headline.

Name_____   **Exercise 20**

SELECTING NEWS

Directions: After you read the following synopses of possible news stories, rank the stories for both news value and significance to *your* community. The story with the highest news value would be ranked number one, the next would be number two, and so on. Also, what news elements dominate each summary?

NEWS VALUE RANK　　　　**STORY**

1. A garage fire in your town this morning claimed the life of Bill Peters, a 19-year old friend of yours, and caused $28,000 damage to the building and its contents.

   _____　　Significance: _____

2. In a special meeting this morning, the city council passed the current year budget.

   The new budget will require an increase in taxes estimated at 30 cents per $1,000. This means that the owner of a property assessed at $40,000 will pay about $12 more in property taxes this year than last.

   _____　　Significance: _____

3. Your local university will receive a federal government grant of $2.5 million to help develop specialized programs for the handicapped. Your school was the only one in your state to receive such a grant.

   _____　　Significance: _____

4. Two local college women were attacked by knife-wielding assailants in separate incidents last night. Both escaped serious injury. Both incidents took place near your campus library.

   _____　　Significance: _____

5. Testimony resumed today in circuit court in a suit brought by your university to determine liability for $21,629.43 in illegal long-distance phone calls made from the municipal building last year.

   _____　　Significance: _____

Name_____ **Exercise 21**

SELECTING NEWS 2

Directions: Suppose you are managing editor of your campus newspaper. After you read the following synopses of possible news stories, rank the stories for both news value and significance to *your* campus. The story with the highest news value would be ranked number one, the next would be number two, and so on. Also, what news elements dominate each summary?

NEWS VALUE RANK **STORY**

1. Despite what may appear as poor sanitation conditions at some of the local bars and restaurants near your campus, they all have fairly clean health records, according to your local board of health.

   _____ Significance:_____

2. The sports information director at your school has accepted a similar position at another school in your state. No one will replace him because of a lack of funds.

   _____ Significance:_____

3. Twenty-two students are gaining a better understanding this term of the role of the family in a communications in the family class. The class instructor stresses basic communications' skills such as family intimacy, listening and love.

   _____ Significance:_____

4. Final rehearsals are beginning for the third production of "The Sound of Music." The Rogers and Hammerstein musical will start next Monday for three days. All students may obtain free tickets if they have valid ID cards.

   _____ Significance:_____

5. Cats are overrunning your campus. Unclaimed cats and kittens have been seen and found in nearly every building on your campus in the last two days. Administrators, faculty and students are baffled about their appearances. More than cats have been caught by campus security.

   _____ Significance:_____

Name_____ **Exercise 22**

Directions: Edit and write a 2-30-2 headline for a 6-column paper.

MANSLAUGHTER

Director Harry Randall, charged with manslaughter, insisted outside a Central Valley courtroom Wed. that the crash was "an unforseeable accident." He was at the hearing which will decide whether he and 4 others should stand trial on involuntary manslaughter.

The accident to which he refers was the death of a child in the filming of the movie, Night Zone. The parents testified about the accident with tears in their eyes that the director shouted, 'Lower, lower.' to the helecopter that crashed into the victims.

The father and his wife of the child have recently been naturalized and changed their name from Le to Lee.

Although the lawyers disputed Dr. Samuel Lee's recollection, he still remained steadfast. "I heard someone saying, Lower, lower. It was Harry Ranall's voice". He instructed the pilot through a megaphone during the fatal filming of a Korean War sequence.

Moments later, the explosions went off and the helicopter crashed. His seven-year old son, Mi Le was decapitated. This was part of his testimony in the trial to decide whether involuntary manslaughter charges should go to trial. His 6 year old child and actor Sam Weber were killed on July 23 1982.

###

Name_____ Exercise 23

Directions: Edit and write a 2-24-2 headline for a 6-column paper.

SCHOOL BOARD

Central Valley school district will hold its regular school board meeting Monday at 7:30 p.m., in the board Room of the Administrative Services Center.

The school boar plans to discuss distribution of anti-drug literature to elementary and junior high school students in the district schools, and will consider bids on four new school buses for the area.

Board appointees for a study committee on athletics will be considered at the meeting, and discussion of food services to district schools is also planned.

Resignations from the district's teaching staff will be considered by the board which will also consider purchase of educational equipment for two area schools.

Consideration on lowering of the junior high school mathematics requirements is being planned and the board will also decide on the allowing and extending of supplemental budgets for certain educative needs.

###

Name _____ **Exercise 24**

Directions: Edit and write a 1-18-3 headline for a 6-column format.

NICARAGUA

In Nicaraqua, the leftist governments defense ministry said it's forces along the border of Nicargua fired Wednesday on an unidentified military helicopter" violating Nicaraguan airspace. The ministries' communique said the aircraft made a forced landing in the neighborhood of two hundred yds. inside Honduras, but it did not mention the pilots death.

A US army pilot was killed by "hostile fire" form this Nicaraquan fire when their helicopter forced a landing in Honduras. The cash was near the border region of Honduras, the capital of Nicaraqua. Cia-backed anti-Sandinista rebels are active there, say US officials.

This was the first reported shooting episode which was the cause of a US casualty since joint US Honduran military maneuvers began in late August.

###

Name_____ **Exercise 25**

Directions: Edit and write a 2-24-2 headline for a 6-column format.

RETREAT

In an interesting item about speeches — that is, if you want to hear "How Liable for Libel?", It will be the lecture subject of Dr. Louis Retreat, Professor of mass communications and director of Student Publications at Central Valley University.

On Wednesday, May 19, at 7:30 p.m. in the evening the public is invited to attend the presentation which will be held in the auditorium in the student center, according to an announcement made today by the chairman of the program.

The chairman additted that he knew that this event was sponsored by a committee of graduate students in the journalism students. "Because of the need for enlightenment as to the extent of the responsibility of the press and the legal limits to which journalists are protected by law, the session is especially open to students of journalism, members of the news media and of the bar association," said the chairman of the progrzm.

This is no admission charge or reservation necessary to attend this program, according to the previous announcement, and an informal discussion and coffee hour will follow the lecture.

###

Name_____ **Exercise 26**

Directions: Edit and write a 2-24-2 headline for a 6-column paper.

MORRISON FIRE

On Sunday, an early morning fire was the cause of extensive damage to a building. The building was 100 years old. It houses the Morrison Town Hall and the Morrison Opera Company. This wooden structure will be rebuilt.

"This isn't going to hurt us," said the respected Morrison major, Rolf Paul. "Less than 50% (of the building) has been damaged, and we will rebuild."

The flaming blaze broke out Sunday morning about 1 a.m. Apparently, the cause was electrical heat tape which was at fault. The heat tape was wrapped around water pipes below the first-floor foyer, said Bill Whitehead, the opera's artistic coordinator.

Firefighters from the Morrison Fire department responded. They extinguished the fire before it could spread to other parts of the building or nearby structures.

The foyer was gutted out, and the staircase was heavily damaged.

###

Directions: Edit and write a 1-18-2 headline for a 6-column paper.

ATHENS

An Athens Seismological Institute spokesman said a tremor occurred at 5:45 am in Greece. The quake measured 4.6 on the Rickter scale.

The medium strength earthquake shook southwestern Greece today but there was no immdiate reports of causalties or damage, the Athens Seismological Institute said.

###

Name _____ **Exercise 27**

Directions: Write a 1-18-3 headline for an 8-column paper after editing the story.

ROSER

Because alert police officers recognized his brilliantly colored plaid wool cap from a previous hold up, Robert R. Roser, 4849 Sheboygan Avenue, was arrested yesterday just as he was about to hold up and rob the University Inn.

Patrolmen John Baum and Jim Foster, who were pasing in their police squad car, happened to look in through the glass doors of the business as they went by and recognized Roser's cap. It was the same one at which they had taken two shots only three hours before when its owner held up the nearby Washington Hotel at 636 W. Washington Avenue. The bandit in the right red cap made his getaway then however.

The two policemen parked their squad car and rushed into the University Inn where they took Roser into custody. He had a fully loaded automatic pistol secreted in his pocket. He admitted having robbed the business earlier. He will be brought before the dectective bureau lineup tomorrow.

###

Name_____   **Exercise 28**

Directions: Edit and write a 3-36-1 headline for a 6-column paper.

FATAL SHOOTING

LOUISVILLE (AP) — Sunday, Louisville police began the investigation of the fatal shooting of a 19-year old man and the stabbing death of a 20 year old. The tow homicides apparently are unrelated.

Leo Sanchez, 19, of 1800 West 44th Avenue, received a shot in the chest shortly after midnight Sunday morning in the 3100 block of West Conejos Place. The incident occured when Sanchez and an acquaintance had a struggle over a .22 caliber handgun.

Freinds of Sanchez rushed him to Saint Anthony Hospital. There, he was pronounced dead shortly after his arrival.

After questioning the witnesses, Timothy Ortiz, who is 19, was arrested by police. The arrest took place at his residence at 4285 Kendall Street in Lexington.

Ortiz is being held in the Jefferson County Jail fro the investigation of homicide. Pending the filing of charges, the police will transfer him to the Louisville City Jail.

Louisville homicide Detective Ervin Haynes said Sanchez, who was a friend of Ortiz, wanted to make an examination of the handgun. Ortiz refused to allow Sanchez to look at the gun. A struggle followed, during which the gun went off.

"It remains to be seen if the district attorney will want to file charges," Haynes said. "But one of the reasons Ortiz is in jail is because he didn't stick around for us and we had to go and arrest him."

###

Name_____ **Exercise 29**

Directions: Edit and write a 2-30-2 headline for a 6-column paper.

RR CRASH

   CHEYENNE (UPI) — Four cars of the Union pacific railroad freigh train leaped over the tracts Today near Cheyenne, Wyoming, and crashed into two buildings.

   The freightened cars also jumped into several parked car in a nearby parking lot. Cheyenne police said that the buildings and the cars were damaged and that no one was injured as the cars and the buildings were not occupied at the time of the when the crash occurred.

   However, the train accident kicked a rear and side wall out of one of the buildings which demolished the White Park Grill. That building was valued at $100,000. Damages to the cars amounted to $20,000, and the damages to the other building totaled $30,000.

   Dick Sadler, a spokesman for the railroad, who also was a foreman, said that the a railroad switch apparently had been left open. The accident occurred when the train cars were backing into a side track.

   This crash is the first one in 14 months for the railroad. Fourteen months ago a quick passenger train jumped the tracks at the same place, and injured 30 persons, and killed two others.

   ###

Name_____ **Exercise 30**

Directions: Edit and write a 2-30-2 headline for an 8-column paper.

PRESTON

Mrs. Louise Preston, eighty-eight, of 515 Peterson, who died two months ago on the first left an estate of one hundred fifty thousand dollars, according to papers filed today in probate court.

Mrs. Preston, the wife of the late B. L. Preston, was a granddaughter of Eben Peck, the first white settler in Collins County. Mrs. Preston willed her ½ interest in land in San Juan County, New Mexico, as follows:

Andrew Leith, Philadelphia, agent for beneficiaries of Mary Leith, ½ interest; and Mark K. Page, Mt. Dora, Florida, and Alice K. Bagg, Junction City, Kansas, ¼ each.

Sums of five hundred dollars each were left to Saint John's Episcopal home, Central Valley, the masonic foundation, and Colorado Easter seal society.

Mrs. Earl Langley, El Canjun, California, and Clarence Cary, Rockford, Illinois, each will receive ten thousand dollars. Sums of $5000 each were left to Phil and Hazel Branch, Longmount, Colorado.

Ronald Harris, 617 Peterson, and Penny Kendall, 423 Westwood, were willed one thousand dollars each.

Amounts of five hundred dollars each went to Mary A. Nelson, Crowley, Louisianna; Mrs. Bert Anderson, Rt. 1, Greenville; Martha Lewis, Madison, Wisconsin; Agnes Hougas, Crystal Lake, Illinois, and Velma Quigley, 2401 Lake Street.

After a number of one hundred dollar bequests Mrs. Preston directed that twenty-five thousand of the remainder of her estate go to the Central Valley Community College to establish a Preston scholarship Fund, and that the rest go to St. Luke's Episcopal church, Central Valley, for its endowment fund.

###

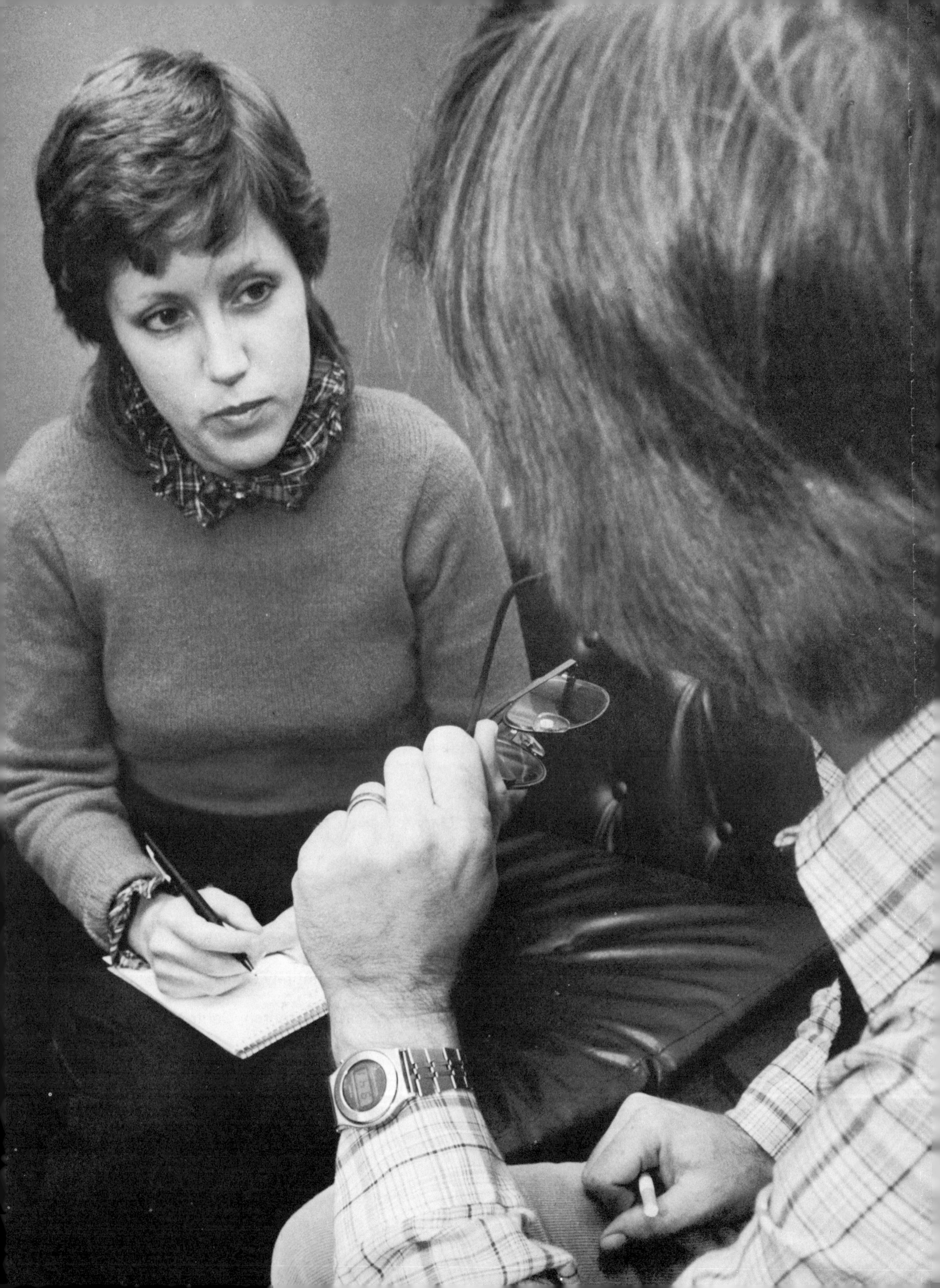

Chapter 6

Handling Features and Special Stories

Features are "soft news," stories about people and things that interest people. They are stories your audience can feel something about and become involved in — stories that entertain and inform. They help keep life in perspective by showing us how other people cope with life, and sometimes they remind us that life isn't all bad news, after all.

An old man living in Space Age America still farms with horses just outside New York City. A lion tamer takes his cats to lunch at a drive-in hamburger stand. Whatever became of all the bomb shelters that were constructed in back yards in the frenzied 50s? How does the old-age pensioner get along without electricity in her home? Such subjects are the heart of a good feature. Consider, for example, the following news story and then see how it might be treated as a feature story.

Straight News Story

Figures released today by the Federal government show that inflation rose another one and one-half percent last month, for an annual rate of 18 percent per year. Officials say the biggest inflationary gains occurred in housing costs, up nearly 14 percent since the beginning of the year. Officials say that at current rates of inflation, single-family dwellings may soon be priced beyond the incomes of most middle-class Americans.

Feature Story

For the last four months, the James Casey family has been camped in this tent just outside Philadelphia. With four children to feed and more than a thousand dollars in unpaid bills . . . James Casey is among more than eight million unemployed Americans.

Disaster overtook the Caseys in a series of measured steps. First, auto sales fell off at the assembly plant where Casey worked as a journeyman welder. That led to temporary layoffs. The Caseys fell behind in their house payments. Then serious illness struck their youngest child. The medical bills grew. And then one day, Casey opened an envelope at work. It contained his final check and a notice of termination. The Caseys lost their house and each day they hope against hope that a new job will come along. For now their tent is home. They can afford no other, and at nightfall when the kerosene lamps are lit, the Caseys know the true meaning of what it is to hear that once again last month . . . inflation rose another one and one-half percent or 18 percent a year.

The basic difference in the two stories is one of approach. The first story has a standard news approach that tells about inflation in abstract figures. The second approach, the feature story, tries to evoke some human emotion as it focuses on a single family to illustrate the consequences of inflation. The copy editor must be careful to preserve the feature qualities while attempting to edit the copy creatively. To turn a straight news story into a feature, you may need to rewrite the lead, the entire story, or send it back to the reporter. The good copy editor, though, should be alert to feature possibilities.

SPECIAL STORIES

"Special" story types demand different treatment by the copy editor. Larger news organizations sometimes handle such stories through a separate copy desk. For instance, sports, family living (society), religion and business stories might be edited by the editor of that department.

Obits:

The obituary is a news story, and should be written as such. It generally includes four major points: who died, what his background is, who the survivors are, and what the funeral arrangements are. Emphasis should be on who died. The phrase, "after a long illness," may be sufficient for explaining the death of an elderly person. However, if a younger person dies of a sudden heart attack, the cause of death is worth mentioning. Newspapers' style differs on the designation of the surviving wife. Some still refer to her as wife, while others consider her the widow (for the Central Valley Free Press, you should use wife). Unless there are few survivors, the grandchildren usually are not named. No adequate substitute exists for the simple word "died." Such phrases as "passed away," "gone on to the Great Beyond," and "called to his eternal reward," do not belong in an obituary. Finally, a body is termed a body, not corpse, remains, or the deceased. The body rests in a coffin, not a casket, and it is buried, not interred. Metropolitan dailies today publish little information about the deceased and that information usually appears in the classified ad section as a paid announcement. Birth announcements are handled in the same way. Obits appearing in suburban dailies and in suburban dailies and in weeklies contain much more information and are written as a news story.

Society:

Other story types involving the human interest aspects of life, such as society news or accidents, also demand special attention. Society news may include such stories as births, organizational activities, social events, weddings, trips, and illnesses. Checking names, identifications and dates are your principal concerns in editing society news.

Accidents:

In accident stories, as with society stories, you must be extremely careful to check and double check the facts, names and addresses. News judgment of the reporter and editor should dictate that the most important element of the accident story usually is loss of life or injury to individuals involved.

Sports:

Sports writers have more freedom of comment and style than the regular news writer, but sometimes sports writers cause problems for the editor. While such comment may cover a wider range than the normal news story, it must not go beyond the bounds of fair comment. For example, a law suit may arise because a sports writer enters into the athlete's privacy by noting in a story that a certain marital problem caused the player to perform poorly. Sports writers also must not overstep their freedom in the use of slang or the vernacular. It may be currently desirable for the writer to use such words and phrases as "rhubarb," "won the toss" and "struck out," but only an amateur would say "booted the pigskin," "scorched the cinders," or "banged the old apple."

Specialties:

In recent years metropolitan dailies have hired specialists to cover news in medicine, religion, environment, consumer items, agriculture, petro-chemical, business and other subjects that are important to their areas. Petro-chemical news is important for those people living in Southeastern Texas and Southern Louisiana because the areas are major petro-chemical centers. Although specialized stories require expertise, you should be familiar with the common terms used by your paper's specialists and be able to translate those technical items into everyday language.

COMPOSITE STORY

When a story has many incidents and angles, it is called a composite story to distinguish it from the simple, one-incident news article. While several reporters and rewrite people may work on the story, it generally is written by one individual reporter or put together by a copy editor. For example, a simultaneous state and local police raid on illegal gambling activities within the country would likely have several story angles involved. Depending on the staff available the angles may be covered by different reporters or by one reporter. In any case the story would be compiled by one person.

The reporter usually will begin his composite story with a comprehensive lead, and sometimes may feature one of the main story elements. In editing the composite story it is the copy editor's responsibility to see that the lead is not "buried" by the reporter, that all angles of the story are fully explained, and that there are no contradictions in the story.

Name_____ **Exercise 31**

Directions: Edit and write a 3-36-1 headline for a 6-column paper.

RODEO CLOWN

Kelly Perkins wears a funny face everyday, oversized, baggy pants, and a large red hat makes people laugh. However to a certain group of young men and women Perkins is taken very, very seriously and may prove to be a lifesaver more than once. Kelly Perkins is a radeo clown. And he earns his living the hard way.

"Its a challenge to me," said the 32 year old cowgirl from Oklahoma City, Oklahoma. "I like to try stuff, sometimes I get caught and some times I get bye," she added.

Perkins first got started, she said, in clowning by working a college rodeo while she was an undergraduate student at Oklahoma State University. "I just got into it and really lik the action," she said. The small clown, she's five feet one, added "when I first started fighting bulls, everytime I turned around I was on the ground." It was sure different being chased by bulls than by men."

After clowning around and bull fighting for the last seven years for money, the Oklahoma native and resident siad that "Bullfighting is mainly instinct, coordination, and reaction, you can't really plan." And, futhermore, the clown stressed, "You never quite learning, there is more to learn all the time.

Perkins said that she works between 40 to 50 rodeos a year, travelling about 60,000 miles. So far in the last six months, she's clowned rodeos throughout Texas, Oklahoma, Louisiana, Alabama, Nebraska, and Colorado.

Each clown uses the same face all the time, Perkins added. She said each comedy act she does takes sometimes weeks to learn depending upon the skills needed and how involved she wants it to be. Most of her own acts are what she termed "fill ins" between the different rodeo events. "I consider myself a rodeo clown who specializes in making people laugh while I'm working."

— 30 —

Directions: Edit and write a 2-24-2 headline for a 6-column paper.

DOLL HOSPITAL

Dolls get sick, to, and doll-doctor Katherine Jacobs runs a clinic or hospital for them.

Mrs. Jacobs' granddaughter broke her doll last summer and there was nowhere in Central Valley to have it repaired.

Mrs. Jacobs decided then and there that she would learn to fix dolls herself for other people. "When my own daughters used to break their dolls, they usually had to be thrown away. I decided that I didn't want to go through years of that sort of thing again," she said.

So Mrs. Jacobs took a mail-order course in doll repairing from Uptime Careers correspondence school. The course normally takes two years, but Mrs. Jacobs said that she was so enthusiastic she completed it in two months.

The Anne Doll Hospital opened it's doors two months ago in the remodelled garage of Mrs. Jacob's home on 127 Sherry Place.

Assorted drawers of arms, legs, and eyeballs line the wall of the workroom. Paintpots and mangled bodies in various stages of repair complete the picutre of controlled chaos.

Each patient is given her own colorful carboard box with a flowered towel mattresses. The doctor talks to her patients while she works.

Mrs. Jacobs, 55, can repair cracked limbs, replaced missing parts, sew new hair onto a doll's scalp, and rejuvenate antique bodies. Mrs. Jacobs said that she regular visits garage sales to find old dolls. She buys discarded dolls whenever and whereever she can find them, and either uses them for the parts, or restores them for sale.

The Anne doll Hospital is holding opening house this Saturday and Sunday from 12 noon to 5 p.m.

Name_____   **Exercise 33**

Directions: Edit the story and write a 2-30-2 headline for an 8-column paper.

JENKINS

Jerry J. Jenkins, of 6212 Summit Ridge Dr., died suddenly this morning at the home of his brother, Sam, who lives in Mount Vernon, Texas, according to word received here. He ha been visiting his brouther when he succumbed to heart failure. Mr. Jenkins has been proprietor of the Campus Shop on College Avenue for 32 years. He was seventy years of age.

Mr. Jenkins was born on Longmount, Colo. He moved to Central Valley and opned the campus shop shortly after World War Two. During taht war he served in the army and was statione at Ft. Bliss near El Paso, Texas. He was an actibe member of the local American Legion Post #232.

Mr. Jenkins body will be shipped back to Central Valley tomorrow. Rev. Dave Akers of the First United Methodist Church will officiate. Other details will be announced later.

Mr. Jenkins leaves his widow, the former Ross Ann Gerdes, and one son, Jerry Jr. 1616 S. Oak Street Central Valley.

###

Name_____ **Exercise 34**

Directions: Edit and write a 1-24-3 headline for an 8-column paper.

NUNN CRASH OBIT

Anne Nunn who graduated from Central Valley Community High School ten years ago this past June was killed Friday evening while driving her 1984 Toyota in downtown Central Valley. Nunn was born in Cnetral Valley on June 23, 1955 and was a clerk at Central Valley Community Hospital.

Her friends labored through the night at Central Valley Community Hospital to save her after the accident. They administered 30 pints of blood and spent three and one-half hours in surgery before Nunn succumbed at 5 a.m. Saturday morning.

A 1983 Ford pickup truck with a camper on it struck and crashed into the Toyota on the driver's side. Miss Nunn's passenger, Bobby Fowler, 16, escaped with minor injuries and bruises.

Julia Gibbs McGee of 5512 Settler said police issued a summons to the other drive. Julia is the mother of Nunn.

Nunn was born in Central Valley on June 23, 1955 at 11 p.m. in the evening, and attended Central Valley High School. She later attended Central Valley Community College after her high school years. She loved people and animals. She found her work at the hospital very satisfying. Besides her mother, she leaves her stepfather, Daniel C. McGee of 5512 Settler Ave., and a stepbrother, Robert J. of 5512 Settler.

Rev. Keith Whitney of the hospital conducted services at St. Thomas Episcopal Church followed by burial in Central Valley Community Cemetary.

Name_____ **Exercise 35**

Directions: Edit the story and write a 1-18-2 headline for an 8-column paper.

PINION

Funeral services for the late Dirk J. Pinon of Grover, retired rancher who passed away after a long and serious illness at the Central Valley Memorial Hospital here, was performed in the family residence in Grover today at 3 p.m. Reverend Stephen L. Cutter of the Grover Baptist Church officiated at the memorial services commemorating Mr. Pinon. Internment was in the Grover Valley cemetery, Grover, Reynolds Funeral Home in charge of arrangements.

Mr. Pinion has lived in Grover all of his life. Before he retired he was engaged in the practice of ranching. In the last few years before his fatal illness which ended in his death, he had been unable to carry on his ranching interests because of failing health.

He was amember of the Baptist Church congregation in Grover and was sixty-eight years old.

Mr. Pinon leaves his wife, Susan, and one brother, Larry of Central Valley.

###

Directions: Write a 1-18-3 headline for an 8-column paper after ending the story.

SMITHERMAN ACCIDENT

Three persons were injured when automobiles driven by Simon N. Lucus, 67 years of age, of 318 West Smith Avenue, and John C. Smitherman, 37 years of ago, of 6062 West 77th Street were in a collision at Oak and Shields streets yesterday afternoon.

Smitherman was issued a traffic citation for driving without a valid driver's license and running a stop sign.

The three injured were taken to central Valley Hospital. Lucus and Smitherman were treated for minor cuts and released, but Sam J. English of 1782 South Roosevelt Street suffered a mild concusion. He was hosptialized overnight for observation. English, 28, was a passenger in the Smitherman car.

###

Name_____   **Exercise 36**

Directions: Edit the following story and write a 1-24-3 head for a 6-column paper.

COLLISION

A two-car collision occured last night about midnight at the intersection of Harvard and Remington Street causing total destruction of one car and damaging a utility pole.

Eugene J. Foster, 32, of 31 Western Pl., died two hours after the collison from head injuries received when his car went out of control and struck a truck drived by Jim J. Skiller.

His death was the fifth trafic fatality in Collins County this year.

Foster apprently had been drinking and went through a stop sign without slowing down. Dan Skitt, 8213 Harvard, a witness to the accident, said the Foster car failed to stop for the stop sign.

The car bounced into a ditch, hit a utility pole and knocked Foster from the car. Foster flew through the air for about 50 feet. The utility pole was snapped in two.

Skiller was uninjured.

###

Name _____   **Exercise 37**

Directions: Edit the story and write a 1-18-2 headline for a 5-column paper.

MARKET

NEW YORK — The stock market seemed to be watching and waiting this last week, falling moderately throught the first three days and then steading over the last two sessions.

The Dow Jones Average of 30 inustrials, which was down more than 9.5 points by Wednesday's close recovered 6.8 points Friday an Thursday to finish teh week down 2.7 points at 1241.60.

Brokers said the Middle East Crisis and fears of continuing high interest rates were the causes for the early losses.

"The market ha a fairly sharp rise during the last few weeks and has also run into profit taking," according to Gordon Jones of Feller and Finch Brokers.

Analysts also sited worries about inflation and tight money as market depressents.

Volume for the week on the New York Stock Exchange was a moderate 60,720,000 shares compared with 58.3 million the previous week. The NYSE index of some 1,500 common stocks was off .23 for the week at 54.37. Standard and Poors' 500-stock index fall .65 to 103.43.

Gulf oil was the weekly volume leader, up 1-1/2 at 22-1/4.

Exercise 38

Directions: Edit and write a 2-30-3 headline for an 8-column format.

CARPENTERS

"I think the carpenters held down an excessive increase to help a depressed industry and simulate the economy," a union sopeksman remarked in commenting on the new contract proposal approved tonight by the union carpenters in the Central Valley area.

The new contract, offered by the AGCV)which stands for Associated General Contractors of Central Valley) raises the base rate wag $2.17 over a three-year period. Carpenters now make $8.17 an hour, plus $1.53 in fringe benefits.

The vote, takenat East High School, was 595 for the new contract and 318 opposed.

Kevin Harding, ACGV director, said the carpenter's settlement was "equitable in relationship to the economic conditionwe hve." The new contract provisions, other than the rage increase, are essentially what the carpenters worked four under the previous four years.

The new contract also contains changes requested by the union in shift provisions, late winter startpolicies and information, on check stubs.

The approbal of the new contract ends a twelve week strike and is the first break in the statewide strike by more than 13,000 members of various craft unions.

-30-

Name _____ **Exercise 39**

Directions: Edit and write a 2-30-2 headline for an 8-column paper.

TIGERS

The Sterling Tigers tied for first place in District IIIA came to Central Valley Tuesday night hoping to take over first place against the last place Bears but the hot shoting Bears buried the Tigers as Central Valley High won its second straight game.

The Bears appeared unbeatable in the first quarter with a husting defense that produced steals and a sharp fast break offense that was executed to near perfection. Central Valley lead 12-9 when junior gurad Ben Britton stole the ole apple at half court and drove in for a layup. Mike Becker then drilled a 15 footer as he pulled up on the fastbreak and on the next onslaught down the court he dishes off to Britton for another layup The three straight buckets pulmetted the Bears out to a 18-9 first quarter lead.

Sterling pulled within five 31-25 midway through the second quarter bu the Bears then tossed in eight unanswered points in 42 seconds of action. Rod wickes hit four free throws during that period as the overflow crowd went wild. The Tigers then hit six points to upull to within seven at the half as Central Valley lead 39-32.

Sterling under coach Paul Mittchell controlled the tempo better the second half with precision passing and patient offense Central Valley managed to protect the lead in the fourth quarter, though, as Britton hit four of five baskets from the field and three straight free throws to lead the Bears to the 74-54 win.

"Every game we play we want to improve and do things our way in the first quarter we couldn't do have played better," said John Miller, the Bear coach. "But then we got careless, we were too satisfied with throwing the long pass. Most of their points came from our turnovers that they were causing at midcourt," he said.

###

115

Name_____   **Exercise 40**

Directions: Edit and write a 2-30-3 headline for a 6-column paper.

NO-HITTER

HOUSTON — The first no-hitter of the year came last night as Rex Schimpf pitched is way to a 1-0 win over the Los Angeles Dodgers.

The Houston Astros righthander struck out 12 on the way to his first big league no-hitter. The 22-year old bested his rival Mark Knudson in a brillant pitching duel.

The no-hitter gave him 16 2/3 innings of not allowing a hit. The major league record is 23 innings by Cy Young in 1904.

In his previous outing Schimpt had overwhelmed the Atlanta Braves batters in another close pitching content 2-1 in 12 innings.

Houston Catcher Ray Fosse was elated. "This is my first time to catch a complete no-hitter," he said. "But if I'm around Schimpf long, I'm sure I'll catch more."

The Angels didn't come close to a hit. In fact, they manage only two baserunners — one when Schimpf walked Tony Solaita on a 3-2 pitch with two out in the first inning and the other when struck out to open the eighth buth reached base when the third strike also was a wild pitch.

In 1983 Schimpf was named the National league Rookie of the Year for a 13-7 record and a 2.60 earned run average. He became only the sixth Houston pitcher to strike out 200 batters in one season.

Monday night's no-hitter will have to be remembered a long time by the young pitcher. "I didn't talk to anybody," he said of his conduct in the Astros dugout while on his way to pitching the no-hitter.

It's not a matter of how good a pitcher you are," Schimpf said, "It's a matter of how lucky you are. there are a lot of good pitchers who never get no-hitters."

The 13,400 fans in the Astrodome cheered each pitch Schimpf threw in the ninth inning. After he fell behind on the hitter Bobby Gritch 2-1, Fosse came to the mound to settle him down. He struck him out and quickly retired the last two batters.

###

Name_____ **Exercise 41**

Directions: Edit and write a 2-36-1 headline for a 6-column paper.

MARATHON

BOSTON — Brad Vadar didn't win the Boston Marathon, but you couldn't tell by looking at him.

The 8-year old's smile indicated only some of the happiness the boy felt as he crossed the finish line 85th out of 119 entrants.

Brad was the youngest person ever to finish the Boston marathon.

The youngster has only been training ten weeks. While he was well back in the pack, he was a respectable fourth among the under 18 entrants.

Brad sprinted across the finish line in 4 hours 19 minutes and 17 seconds. The 26 mile, 365 yard course was a short distance for the 49-pounder who logs 80-90 miles a week on the back country roads near his home in Manchester, N.H.

He plans to duplicate his performance here at the Cheyenne Frontier Days marathon this summer in Wyoming.

###

Name_____ **Exercise 42**

Directions: Edit the story and write a 1-18-2 headline for an 8-column paper.

MURPHY

The Central Valley Chamber of Commerce met last night and installed officers.

Installed as president was Mrs. Leonard (Barbara) Murphy, 42, who operates the Ski Shop on Bishop Street with her husband. Following graduation from the University of Kansas where she met her husband, Mrs. Murphy taught English in high school at Springfield, Ill. for 12 years. She and her husband moved to Central Valley 10 years ago and opened the Ski Shop. she is the first woman in the 55-year history of the Central Valley Chamber of Commerce to be elect ed president.

Other officers installed include vise president, Jim Swish, treasurer, James Linoel, and secretary, Ray Kimball.

Featured speaker at the banquet at the Steak House was Clarence Bewley, city manager of Catlinburg, Tenn. He told how the noted tourist center handles its growth and promotion.

###

Exercise 43

Directions: Edit the story and write a 1-24-2 headline for a 6-column paper.

PASTOR

The First Presbyterian church of Central Valley announced today that it will have a high attendance Sunday next week to welcome their new pastor.

Rev. J. J. Snelling resigned to accept a pastorate in Chicago. Snelling left three months ago.

The selection committee for a new pastor included Tim O'Coony, chairman, Fred Sauer, secretary, Carolyn Holland, and Mkie Costello.

Rev. Burke has a wife, Laura, and two children, Cindy and Mark Jr. Cindy is 12 and Mark is 8. They are moving here from Raleigh, N.D. where Rev. Burke was minister at the Homewood Presbyterian church. He had been theree for 9 years after graduating from Princeton Theological Ceminary. He received his B.A. from the University of Indiana in 1958.

The Burkes will live at 303 Indiana Pl. in the chruch manse.

###

Directions: Edit and write a 1-18-3 headline for a 6-column paper.

BISHOP SEES BETTER CHURCH SCHOOLS

MADISON, WI. — The current crisis in catholic education serves as an opportunity to renew and purify the system according to Bishop Cletus F. O!Donnell of the Madison Catholic Diocese.

He said the catholic school system has problems but is basically healthy here.

"The system is faced with 2 basic related problems" O'Donnel said. "One is a lack of religious teachers the other is a lack of finances."

These problems have le to the closing of many schools and reduced operations of others. At least 6 elementary schools now operating in the Madison Diocese will not open again this Fall.

Name_____ **Exercise 44**

Directions: Edit and write a 2-24-1 headline for a 6-column paper.

BAPTIST

OKLAHOMA CITY — Whitehead Baptist Church affliated with the southern Baptist convention in Whitehead, Oklahoma recently ordained three women as ministers. The controversial move breaks Baptist tradition immensely.

Church minister of Whitehead Baptist Church, Ray Gold, said that the women ment all the educational requirements, as well as experience and calling into the ministry.

Because of these ordination, other Oklahoma churches have complained about their authority to do so. But since Southern Baptists promote local church polity, the Whitehead congregation can stand to it's decision.

The ordinations are part of changes effecting the entire Convention and may lead to a confrontation on the floor of the next annual meeting in Kansas City.

Vivian Cole, Shirley Wills, and Fran Harner were the three women for who the church held the ordination service. None were available for comment about the ordination or convention reaction.

Southern Baptists are the largest body of Baptists in the world, claiming a membership of over 12 million people. They have churches in every United States' state and in many countries all over the world.

Directions: Edit and write a 2-30-2 headline for a 6-column format.

YORK

What can happen to a high school valedictorian after he leaves his high school? In the case of Michael York, a senior at Central Valley University, much can happen.

With a 3.79 grade point average, his free spare time is used for studying, Michael noted. Many days, Michael may begin his studying at 5am or stay up till 1am or 2 a.m. for his studying.

Michael received a scholarship from Purina for $500. He is also on the CVU President's Scholarship. He said that when he graduated from highschool, he got a letter form the University tilling him he had got the President's scholar ship for $1500.

Besides his academic performance, extra-cirricular activities also are a major part of Michael's life. He serves as Student Senate Vice President, Bio-agriculture club President, and as a Student ambassador for prospective students and their parents. Micheal also enjoys to sing, playing his guitar, and the writing of music.

How does he do all this? Michael just smiles and says that the people make everything worthwhile. "If I didnt have the extra - cirriculer activitiers, I couldnt do as good with my own studies."

Michael looks to go on into graduate school, focusing on special research in bio-agriculture. He hasn't yet decided where he should go for his graduate work.

"I owe my secess and love for people to my parents and the way they raised me. Without their constent support and encouragement, I wouldn't be where I am now."

Michael is the son of Dr. and Mrs. Randal York of 435 County Club st., and is the oldest of 4 children. The Yorks have lived in Central Valley for the last 9 years. Before then, they resided in Omaha, Nebraska, and in Kansas City, Missouri.

Name_____ **Exercise 46**

COMPOSITE STORY EXERCISE

Directions: You're the news editor of the Central Valley Free Press, our afternoon competitor to the Daily Tribune. As you went home from work last night the wind began to blow. A big wind. Not everyone got to work this morning. Like the Daily Tribune, you have an early edition. A despairing city editor drops this batch of copy on your desk and says: "Looks like I'm not going to have anyone to rewrite this stuff. It isn't in bad shape. I think you can paste it into a round-up story." You have 1½ hours to piece the story together and to write a 6-60-1 head plus 2-36-2 readout.

(FROM THE POLICE REPORTER)

Four persons were injured, none seriously, in automobile accidents, and two others died from electrical shock caused by fallen electrical wires last night as the high winds roared into Central Valley.

City police and Collins country officers attributed all three of the accidents, in which four were injured, to the wind.

Those injured in the car crashes were:

Tom C. Latimer, 221 E. Elm St., arm cuts and bruises, treated at Community hospital.

Susan B. Latimer, his wife, head bruises, treated at Community hospital.

Ben L. Britton, 1020 Patton Avenue, possible internal injuries, taken to Community hospital, condition "good."

James J. Green, 322 S. Grant St., broken arm, treated at Community hospital.

Those who died were:

John K. Hooper, 63, 725 Aster Avenue

David L. Jackson, 70, 425 Princeton Rd.

Mr. Hooper was taken by police ambulance to Community hospital, where he died about two hours after trying to repair a downed electric line on his front porch.

Jackson, retired machinist, dropped dead immediately when an electric pole fell and he stepped on a wire trying to avoid the pole at 8 o'clock last night. He was employed at Smith Implements for thirty-five years.

(Also from police reporter)

City and county work crews were hard at work on Central Valley and Collins county streets and highways this morning, but by noon today only a few major streets were open to cars.

With trees and wires down and other debris scattered over streets and sidewalks, many city people walked or hitch-hiked to work this mornign. Others didn't get to work at all.

At the county office building, department heads estimated that only about 75% of the county employe working force had turned up by 8 a.m. But they added that more and more of the workers arrived as the morning passed.

City police and county traffic officers reported few traffic tie-ups.

"There just isn't much traffic. Most people played it smart and left their cars home," Police Capt. John Holmes said.

Streets superintendent Joseph McLain said that by night fall all major city streets would be cleared. He said that his street crew, number 78 men, would continue to work all night clearning as many side streets as possible.

Many people were grumbling and complaining that the city and coutny crews were mighty slow about getting streets and highways cleared. Several county schools couldn't open because of blocked roads.

(From early phone call taken by office secretary)

City desk:

Mr. Sanders, supt. of schools, called, said Central Valley schools would stay open today. Said less than two-thirds of pupils present, but "there's no sense in sending home those who made it." Said there'd be no penalties against pupils who failed to get there.

Helen

(From phone calls made by the city editor himself)

The Central division of the Automobile Association of America (AAA) warned that only emergency driving shold be attempted on highways in the Central Valley area.

"Every highway leading to Central Valley is badly litered, and we have had reports this morning of 43 cars abandoned within a 50-mile radius of the city," the AAA office said.

It add that highways 34, 14 and 287 plus Interstate 95 were in especially bad shape. The Central Motor Couch line, which uses Highway 287 as part of its Central Valley route, cancelled all runs until later today.

Greyhound officials said that although they had cancelled no trips, "all of our buses arrived and left late this morning."

(from the state editor)

City desk:

Here's a roundup of weather stuff phoned in by country correspondents. Suggest it as insert somewhere in your weather story.

Schools were closed, streets were clogged, and highway traffic was all but halted in most of the Central Valley area this morning.

Strong winds up to 165 mph were reported from Junction on the north to Rockcastle on the south, and from Grand River on the west to Sterling on the east.

Schools were officially closed in the following communities:

Johnstown, Rockcastle, Junction, Grand River, Winter Park, Greenville, Windsor.

Scores of other rural schools were known to have closed without an official announcement.

At Loveland, two city bull dozers and one truck broke down and traffic was at a standstill.

A Central Valley family of four was forced to flee their burning home after a fire blamed on downed power lines caused by the wind.

Elmer Glutz, his wife, Emily, and their two children, Jimmy, 6, and Betty, 2, took refuge with neighbors after their home was completely destroyed by the fire. Their home was located at 616 Court Street.

(From the only general assignments report who came to work)

Winds up to 165 miles an hour and accompanied by freezing temperatures, hit Central Valley and Collins county last night. Two persons died as a result of the storm.

It was the worst wind storm in 35 years to hit Central Valley.

The weatherman said that 90-mile winds prevailed most of the night, with gusts recording as high as 165 miles-an-hour shortly after midnight. They subsided to below 25 mph by 5 a.m. this morning, he said.

Snow is predicted for today, but the weatherman added that "it might only be light flurries."

###

Note: A late call from a reporter at Central Valley University had the following information. Please include information in your roundup.

Gusting winds this morning blew out a plate glass window in the R. G. Smith student center cafeteria injurying two students — Carl Doyle and David Rich.

The students were taken to the student health center where Riche is listed in fair condition with cuts to the face and arms — Doyle is listed in satisfactory conintion withminor cuts.

The educational media tower atop the social science building was blown down about 8:30 this mornining causing an estimated $10,000 damage to the tower and $12,000 to the humanities building which it hit as it fell. Fortunately no won was injured as the tower narrowly missed William matzner as he tried to get to class.

President of Central Valley University, Dr. J. C. Larco, called off classes at 9 a.m. this morning and requested students stay in there dorms or apartments.

-30-

Name_____ **Exercise 47**

COMPOSITE EXERCISE 2

Directions: You are the city editor for the Central Valley Free Press. At 9:05 you receive a call from the police reporter telling you that the Central Valley National Bank has just been robbed of approximately $750,000. You don't know any details yet, but assign reporters to check with the bank president, the FBI office, the police, the teller involved, and any available witnesses.

At 10:10 you receive the first reports and you have to compile them into a composite story by a noon deadline. That means you have 1 hour and 50 minutes to compile the story, edit it, and write a 6-72-1 banner headline for a 6-column paper. You also need a 2-30-2 readout. The copy is on your desk. Get with it.

From General Assignment Reporter

"I thought he would kill us; I didn't think he would let us go," recounted the still shakey bank teller who had been held at gunpoint during today's bank robery.

Ben Manuel, the bank teller, was held by the robber, who forced bank president, Sam Young, to open the vault. Young, said, "I had no choice. The money's not worth a human life." Young, who lives in rural Grover and has been bank president just three months, gave the robber what they wanted — maybe as much as three quarters of a million dollars.

After Manuel and Young carried the sacks of money to the waiting car, the robber let them go. "We just ran back into the bank to see about the man that had been shot," Young said. "The whoel experience seems like a nightmare now," he said. "I just counldn't believe it was happening."

From the police reporter

Central Valey National Bank was held up and robbed of $750,000 this morning about 9:00 A.M. by two bandits, one male and one female.

Two suspects are being sought by police. Warrents have been issued for the arrest of Ron and Danielle Ziegler of Central Valley. Ron was picked out of a mug book by Ben Manuel, bank teller who was held at gun point by Ziegler while he demanded the money from the bank president. The two suspects are thought to be heading toward Wyoming in the interstate highway.

Ziegler is 5'10" tall and weighs about 165 lbs. He has dark brown hair and brown eyes. Danielle is about 5'0" and weighs about 125. Both are 30 years old. Ziegler served three years in the state pen for a 1965 armed robbery of a New Orleans liquor story. The woman drove the getaway car, a green Plymouht.

An off duty policeman, Frank Valdez, was shot in the robbery. All of his friends at the police station are out to get the man who shot Frank.

According to Manuel, a man entered the bank as it was opening at 9 o'clock. He came in and went to Manuel's window. The robber pulled a short, black revolver and demanded that Manuel let him into the teller's area. The robber held a gun on Manuel and went to the bank presidetn, Sam R. Young, and demanded that he place all the big bills from the weekend deposits in two large bags. After the money was stuffed in the sacks, Manuel and Young were forced to carry the sacks to the car parked out back. On the way out Frank Valdez tried to stop the robbery and was shot in the shoulder.

-30-

From the FBI (phone call)

All Wagg, local FBI agent, said this morning that theFBI had joined in the search for the two bank robbers. He said agents in Nebraska and Wyoming had been alerted to watch for two suspicts thought to be heading north.

While Wagg refused to disus details of the investagation, he indicated that their were several leads in the case including two suspects.

From the police captain (phone call)

John Holmes, Central Valley police captain and officer in charge of this the robbery investigation, said loss in the robbery could go as high as $750,000 although it is too early to know for sure.

Holmes said an all points bulletin had been issued for the arrest of Ron and Danille Zeigler, suspects in the case.

Sue Walsh, a local resident, said shehad seen a car with occupants meeting the suspects description, speeding as they turned on the interestate highway heading north toward Wyoming. She saw the car about 9:30 A.M. as she was leaving from work at the Holiday Inn. The speeding car nearly hit her as she was trying to leave the Holiday Inn parking lot.

From general assignments reporter

A courageous witness to this mornings bank robbery, Mr. Frank Valdez, tried to stop the robbery, but failed.

Valdiz, an off-duty policemen, was shot in the left shoulder while trying to stop the robbery. He tried to knock the gun from the man as he held a pistol on one of the tellers, Ben Manuel. The robber shot him, though, before he could succeed. He was reported in good condition at Central Valley Hospital after surgury of 45 minutes to remove a 25-calibre slug from his left shoulder.

James Catlin, local business man who was in the bakn at the time of the robbery descied the robber as about medium height with dark hair. He wore heavy black rimmed glasses.

Catlinalso got a glimpe of the bandits as they fled the parking lot. He said a woman was driving the light green 1972 Plymouth Fury that was used as the getaway car. He only saw the first couple of numbers and did not get the letters of the lisense plate. The first two numbers were "54", he said.

-30-

MOVIE SYSTEMS:
ENTERTAINMENT COMMUNICATIONS

NewsRelease

For Release: May 25, 1983   Contact: John A. Stephens

MOVIE SYSTEMS, INC. DELISTED FROM NASDAQ

DES MOINES, IOWA. The common stock of Movie Systems, Inc. has been delisted from the National Association of Securities Dealers' Automated Quotation System ("NASDAQ") because of a failure to meet all of NASDAQ's listing standards. Continued inclusion requires maintenance of capital and

Chapter 7

Publicity Releases

One of the principal sources of information comes to the media in the form of a publicity release. One study of the Milwaukee Journal found that 24 percent of the Journal's non-syndicated material came from publicity releases. Other studies have shown that radio, television and newspapers have from 10 to 30 per cent of their total content in news that came in the form of a publicity or news release.

While the media use publicity releases, they reject many more than they accept. In a study of 61 editors, Prof. James Julian found several common mistakes made in press releases that lead to their rejection. In order of frequency they are as follows:

(1) Limited local interest.
(2) No reader interest at all.
(3) Story poorly written.
(4) Disguised advertising.
(5) Material obviously faked.
(6) Apparent inaccuracy in the story.
(7) Duplication of material.
(8) Material stretched too thin.

You must exercise sound news judgment in evaluating publicity material not only for style, but because it may represent undue emphasis on special-interest points of view. Many times releases and fact sheets will be newsworthy, but may need to be reworked to meet your requirements.

In editing publicity material, check the following guidelines.

1. Is the self-interest point of view unduly emphasized? If so, can it be eliminated?
2. Is the material localized? If not, can it be localized?
3. Is the lead well written to capture the most important aspect of the story? If not, can you rewrite the lead?
4. Is there unnecessary material in the news story? Can you condense it? (Publicity material is often padded.)
5. Does the material correspond to your style? If not, can it be edited to conform?
6. Do you have any questions about the story? If you do, call the contact person whose name should appear on the release. Call collect if the source lives outside your area. The public relations practitioner should be happy to answer your questions.

Name_____ **Exercise 48**

Directions: Cut the Keystone story to 3-5 paragraphs. Choose one photo to accompany the story and write a 3-5 word caption and a 25-50 word cutline. Write a 2-30-1 headline for a six-column newspaper.

Name_____ **Exercise 49**

Directions: Edit the Texas Energies press release and write a 2-24-3 headline for a 6-col. newspaper.

Name_____ **Exercise 50**

Directions: Edit the Tyler Corporation press release. Use dates that correspond to the current situation. Use the last full calendar year as the date of the financial statement. Write a 3-36-1 healine.

news from Keystone

Keystone International, a Division of Ralston Purina Company, Box 38, Keystone, Colorado 80435 303/468-2316

FOR IMMEDIATE RELEASE

MEDIA CONTACT:
Lois Barr
303/468-2316
Ext. 3830

ONE MILLION SKIERS CAN'T BE WRONG!
COLORADO'S SUMMIT COUNTY HAS IT ALL

SUMMIT COUNTY, Colo.--It is not merely by chance that Summit County, Colorado, has become the most popular ski complex in the country, for the past three seasons drawing more than one million skiers to its multitude of slopes.

Thirty-eight lifts, 180 miles of trails and bowls, a lift capacity of 48,850 skiers per hour and 8,703 vertical feet of skiing didn't just happen.

Summit County's four resorts, two of them among the oldest in Colorado and two of them among the newest, have been perfecting the ski experience for quite sometime. Together, they span a skiing history of more than 30 years.

The four are Keystone, Copper Mountain, Breckenridge and Arapahoe Basin, Ski the Summit's newest addition. In the 1940s, a few "die-hards" brought their wooden skis, their lace boots and their sack lunches to Arapahoe Basin and skied its vast, alpine bowl, situated at 12,500 feet, its steep, bumpy slopes and its acres of deep, powder snow. They still go there for the same reasons.

(More)

Ski the Summit
Page 2

Then, almost 20 years later, a new brand of skier brought metal skis, buckle boots and stretch pants to Breckenridge, a resort which has turned yellow gold, mined for years in its streams and mountains, to white gold.

When Keystone came along almost 15 years later, skiers tried short skis and loved them, enjoyed dining elegance and indoor tennis. Then, Copper Mountain added more steep slopes and moguls, plenty of them, and the state's first, covered chairlift.

Today's skier will find all this and more when he visits Summit County's big, four-ring, interconnected ski circus. In addition to the skiing, which includes wide, gentle boulevards, vast, alpine bowls and steep, bumpy pitches, all in abundance, the visitor will discover enough bars and restaurants to keep him busy for a week and snow, the kind you write home about.

And, an added bonus is that Colorado's highest county is located only 72 miles from Denver's busy, Stapleton International Airport on interstate highway. It is easy to get here from there, via I-70, and there are no passes to cross. Once in Summit County, all four resorts are connected by free, convenient shuttle buses.

A Summit County ski vacation can be booked by travel agents in major cities throughout the country. Four-and-six-day Ski the Summit packages are available, and, in some cases, the package qualifies the traveler for a lower, tour-basing airfare.

(More)

Accommodations, for five or seven nights, are available at the resorts themselves or in nearby lodges. The entire county can sleep some 8,000 persons in a variety of facilities, ranging from moderately priced motels to luxurious lodges.

Package prices vary depending on the type of accommodations selected and the number of people. Double occupancy rates could range from $81 to $174 per person for the five-night package and from $135 to $265 per person for the seven-night package. Six people could stay for six nights in motel-type accommodations for as little as $88 apiece.

Packages also include four or six-days' worth of lift tickets which can be used to ski the four areas. However, only one mountain can be skied per day. Lift ticket booklets also can be purchased independently of the packages at all lift ticket windows in the county. If purchased this way they cost $40 for four days and $60 for six.

In Summit County the snows come early and stay late. Colorado's longest season begins in early November and lasts until June. And just to make certain nature has no little tricks up its sleeve, there are 250 acres of all-purpose terrain covered by snow-making.

The youngest member of Ski the Summit, Arapahoe Basin is a true alpine ski complex set in a vast powder bowl above treeline and rimmed by the jagged sweep of the Continental Divide. There, some of the finest spring skiing in the state lasts into June. At 12,500 feet above sea level, the skiing rivals that of the Alps or Bugaboos.

(More)

But only the view need be awesome; there are avenues of descent from this wonderland for the beginner as well as for the expert.

Just five miles down the road is Keystone, skiing's glamour child. Its predominance of gently, rolling terrain complements Arapahoe Basin's steeper slopes, just 10 minutes away. A division of Ralston Purina Co., Keystone is a glittering, year-round resort. Its posh, 152-room Lodge, is highly rated with four stars in the prestigious Mobil Travel Guide, and its contemporary village, which overlooks a three-level Plaza and a lake, radiates both luxury and comfort.

Ski slopes at this contemporary resort range from manicured boulevards to undulating trails which follow the natural terrain. Altogether, Keystone has 40 miles of trails and nine lifts. Two day lodges, one at the base of the mountain, the other at the 11,640-foot summit, serve everything from hamburgers to hearty stews.

In addition to skiing, other Keystone activities include indoor tennis at John Gardiner's Tennis Ranch, figure and speed skating on Keystone Lake, sleigh rides and swimming - in 12 pools scattered throughout the complex.

Another 15 miles via Interstate 70 and U.S. 6, brings one to Copper Mountain, often called the most perfect ski mountain in the Rockies. Experts can romp through the steep bumps of the World Cup courses on the east side of the area, while beginners can practice their snowplows on the forgiving west runs. In the center is a broad expanse of scintillating intermediate terrain which captures the best of both worlds.

(More)

Copper's base area, which boasts some interesting bars and restaurants for apres-ski enjoyment, lives up to its name. Its buildings are made of sheet steel to rust to a pleasant brown-copper color.

This winter, Copper Mountain will add 82 acres of snowmaking and a new "J" lift which will service two new intermediate trails on the right side of the mountain. The Yan double chairlift will be 5,110 feet long.

From Copper Mountain, Breckenridge lies 15 miles south off Colorado 9. A pleasant, giant of a mountain, Breckenridge has 14 lifts situated on Peaks 8 and 9 of the Ten Mile Range and two separate base areas. Most of the terrain is rolling and gentle, but there are a few surprises - such as discovering a vertical chute, which happens to be the steepest run in the state.

In contrast to the skiing, the Kingdom of Breckenridge is rustic and old, a remnant left over from mining days. And indeed, it was a kingdom, for in 1936, it was discovered that in all its myriad land acquisitions, the nation somehow had neglected a 1,300-square-mile tract with the little town as its center. Some long-time residents still are sorry the town bothered to join the union.

A world of its own, Breckenridge's Victorian architecture is sprinkled with a variety of slab-sided, tin-roofed relics from the mining days. Numerous restautants and hideaway shops now occupy these delightful old buildings which have been restored to provide an aura of comfort and antiquity.

########

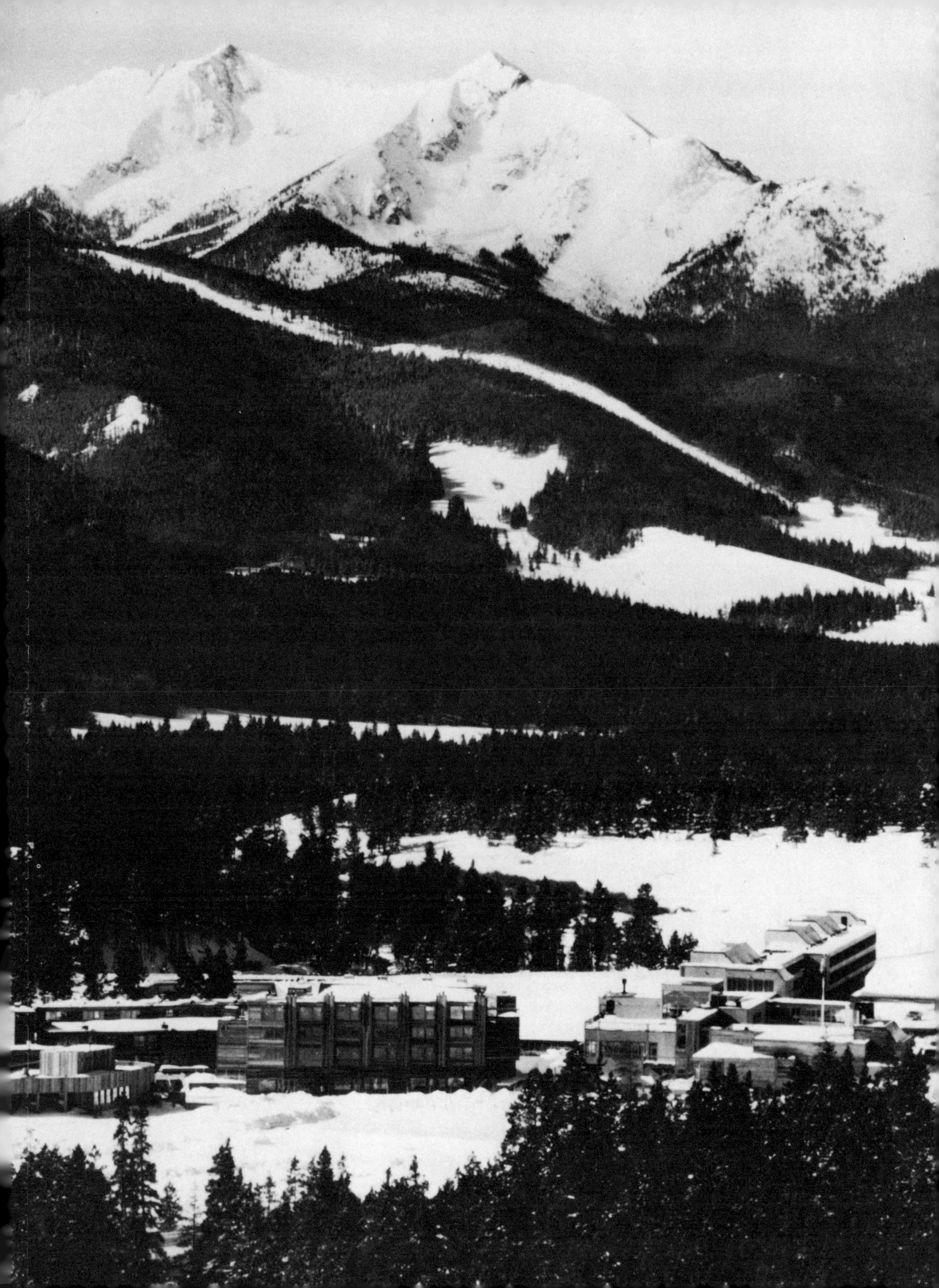

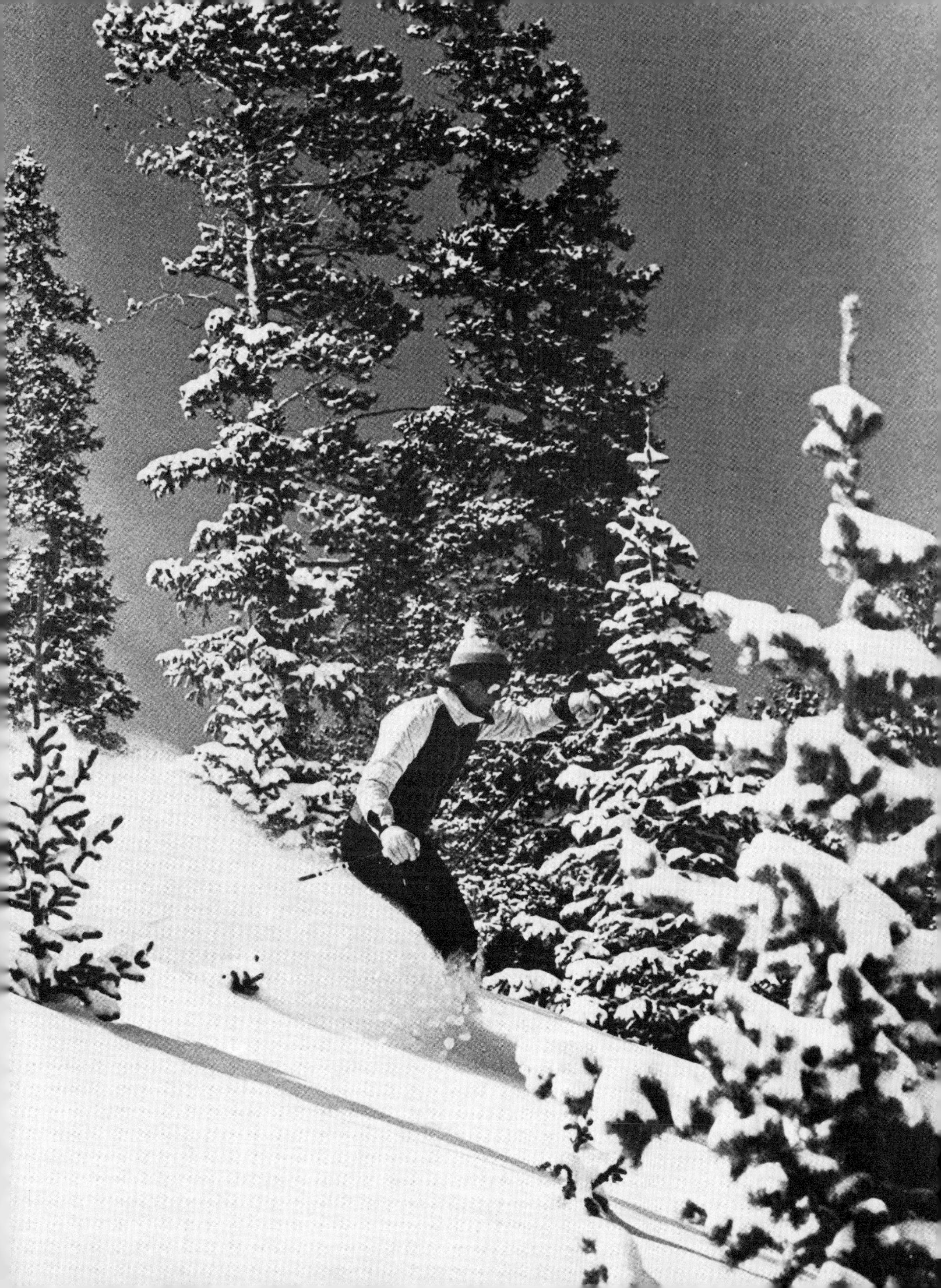

TEXAS ENERGIES, INC.
PRESS RELEASE

For Immediate Release
NASDAQ Trading Symbols:
   TXEN, Common
   TXENU, Units
   TXENW, Warrants

Contact: Rhonda Roe
         Public Relations Coordinator
         P.O. Box 947
         Pratt, Kansas 67124
         (316) 672-7581

Or: Mike Engleman
    The Engleman Company, Inc.
    7557 Rambler Road #819
    Dallas, Texas 75231
    (214) 691-4161

TEXAS ENERGIES ANNOUNCES
SUCCESSFUL DRILLING RESULTS

PRATT, Kansas, June 7, 19 ...Texas Energies, Inc. (NASDAQ/TXEN) today announced successful exploration and drilling activities for the prior two months. The Long #1-5, a Pratt County, Kansas development well is currently producing 70 barrels of oil per day from the Mississippian Formation after fracture treatment. This well, located between two major oil and gas producing trends, was successful in Texas Energies' effort to continue exploring and developing 22,000 acres of leases in Northeast Pratt County. The initial well, the Huff #1-8, also extended Mississippian production in the area. Seismic surveys taken across the remaining acreage indicate excellent potential for further development. Texas Energies is the operator and holds a 75.5% working interest.

The Mann #1-21, Stafford County, Kansas, showed positive indications during testing. A drill stem test run in the Pennsylvanian Conglomerate recovered gas to surface in 30 seconds, stabilizing at a rate of 5.69 million cubic feet of gas per day. Immediate completion of this exploratory well is planned and gas sales should commence within 60 days after completion. The Mann #1-21 is part of Texas Energies' 198 Winter Drilling Program. Of the 12 exploratory prospects in this program, 11 have been drilled and completion of the program is expected by June 15. The Company owns a 27.5% working interest in this program with the remaining interest held by industry partners and private investors.

-more-

TEXAS ENERGIES, INC.
PRESS RELEASE

Drilling--2

Another significant gas discovery was reported in Barber County, Kansas. Three productive gas zones were encountered during drill stem testing on the Ash #1-26. During testing in the Lansing Formation, the well was gauged at an initial rate of 2.31 million cubic feet of gas per day on a 2-inch choke with flowing tubing pressure of 230 psi. The Ash is currently producing into a gas sales line at the rate of 460,000 cubic feet per day. The Company owns a 25% working interest in this well.

In addition, the Company has expanded operations on its Hoagland-Hinz acreage in Barber County, Kansas. Texas Energies has drilled 9 wells in this area, of which 4 are oil wells, 4 are gas wells and an additional oil well is waiting on completion. The Hinz #1-26, an exploratory well located on this acreage, has been completed in the Mississippian. During initial testing gas was gauged at 2.3 million cubic feet per day from four feet of perforations. Future completion attempts will be made in the Marmaton and Elgin Formations. The well is located approximately 1 1/2 miles from other production. Texas Energies is the operator and owns a 35% working interest in these wells and the surrounding acreage.

News

Southland Center
Dallas, Texas 75201, Tel: 214/747-8251

Tyler Corporation

Ben R. Murphy
Vice President

TYLER CORPORATION REPORTS
198 FINANCIAL RESULTS;
INCREASES DIVIDEND

Dallas, Texas, January 30   -- FOR IMMEDIATE RELEASE

Joseph F. McKinney, chairman and chief executive officer of Tyler Corporation (NYSE), reported today that the Company's earnings increased 74% from $1.08 per share in 198 to $1.88 per share in 198 . Net income rose 81% to $18.4 million in 19 Net sales and operating revenues were 10% higher at a record $961 million. Return on assets employed improved from 16% in 19 to 20% in 19 .

McKinney noted that five of Tyler's six operating companies had higher profits in 1983 and that four of the companies had gains in sales.

In the final three months of 19 , earnings per share of $.50 were 100% higher than the $.25 recorded in the fourth quarter of 19 . Net income increased 99% to $4.9 million on a 25% gain in sales to $272 million.

-more-

Tyler Corporation   -2-   January 30

"We are happy to report significant improvements in earnings and return on assets," McKinney said, "but performance cannot be considered satisfactory until earnings begin to exceed the record levels set in 1981. We are extremely pleased with the overall enlargement the operating companies made in their market share in 198 and 198 and believe that these positional moves will make possible resumption of successive earnings records."

Dividend Increased

The board of directors of Tyler Corporation has declared a 1984 first quarter dividend of $.175 per share, increasing the annual cash dividend rate from $.65 to $.70 per share. This represents the eleventh year in a row that dividends have been increased since being instituted in 1973. The first quarter dividend is payable February 20, 198 to shareholders of record on February 7, 1984.

Tyler Corporation, with national headquarters in Dallas, provides goods and services to industrial customers. Its operations include electronic components distribution, specialty chemical coatings, industrial explosives, pipe and fittings and trucking.

(Comparative results follow.)

TYLER CORPORATION

CONSOLIDATED STATEMENTS OF INCOME

(Thousands of dollars, except earnings per share)

	Year ended December 31 198	198	% of Change
Net sales and operating revenues	$960,923	$870,501	+10
Costs and expenses	900,941	823,887	+9
Interest expense	26,438	29,037	-9
Income before income tax	33,544	17,577	+91
Income tax	15,095	7,382	+104
Net income	$ 18,449	$ 10,195	+81
Earnings per common share	$ 1.88	$ 1.08	+74
Average shares outstanding during the period (thousands)	9,812	9,464	

	Three months ended December 31 198	198	% of Change
Net sales and operating revenues	$271,675	$216,490	+25
Costs and expenses	256,218	205,643	+25
Interest expense	6,577	6,620	-1
Income before income tax	8,880	4,227	+110
Income tax	3,996	1,775	+125
Net income	$ 4,884	$ 2,452	+99
Earnings per common share	$ .50	$ .25	+100
Average shares outstanding during the period (thousands)	9,827	9,661	

SALES AND OPERATING PROFITS

(Thousands of dollars)

	198_	198_	% of Change
Net Sales and Operating Revenues			
Atlas Powder	$127,383	$131,025	-3
C & H Transportation	101,587	120,841	-16
Hall-Mark Electronics	242,848	154,608	+57
Reliance Universal	176,680	170,552	+4
Thurston	120,432	113,597	+6
Tyler Pipe	191,993	179,878	+7
	$960,923	$870,501	+10
Operating Profits			
Atlas Powder	$ 7,490	$ 5,529	+35
C & H Transportation	1,829	7,393	-75
Hall-Mark Electronics	13,861	7,062	+96
Reliance Universal	14,533	9,007	+61
Thurston	6,344	3,698	+72
Tyler Pipe	25,249	23,817	+6
	69,306	56,506	+23
Other Expenses			
Subsidiary nonoperating expense	(3,182)	(3,094)	+3
Interest expense	(26,438)	(29,037)	-9
Corporate expense	(6,142)	(6,798)	-10
	(35,762)	(38,929)	-8
Income Before Income Tax	$ 33,544	$ 17,577	+91

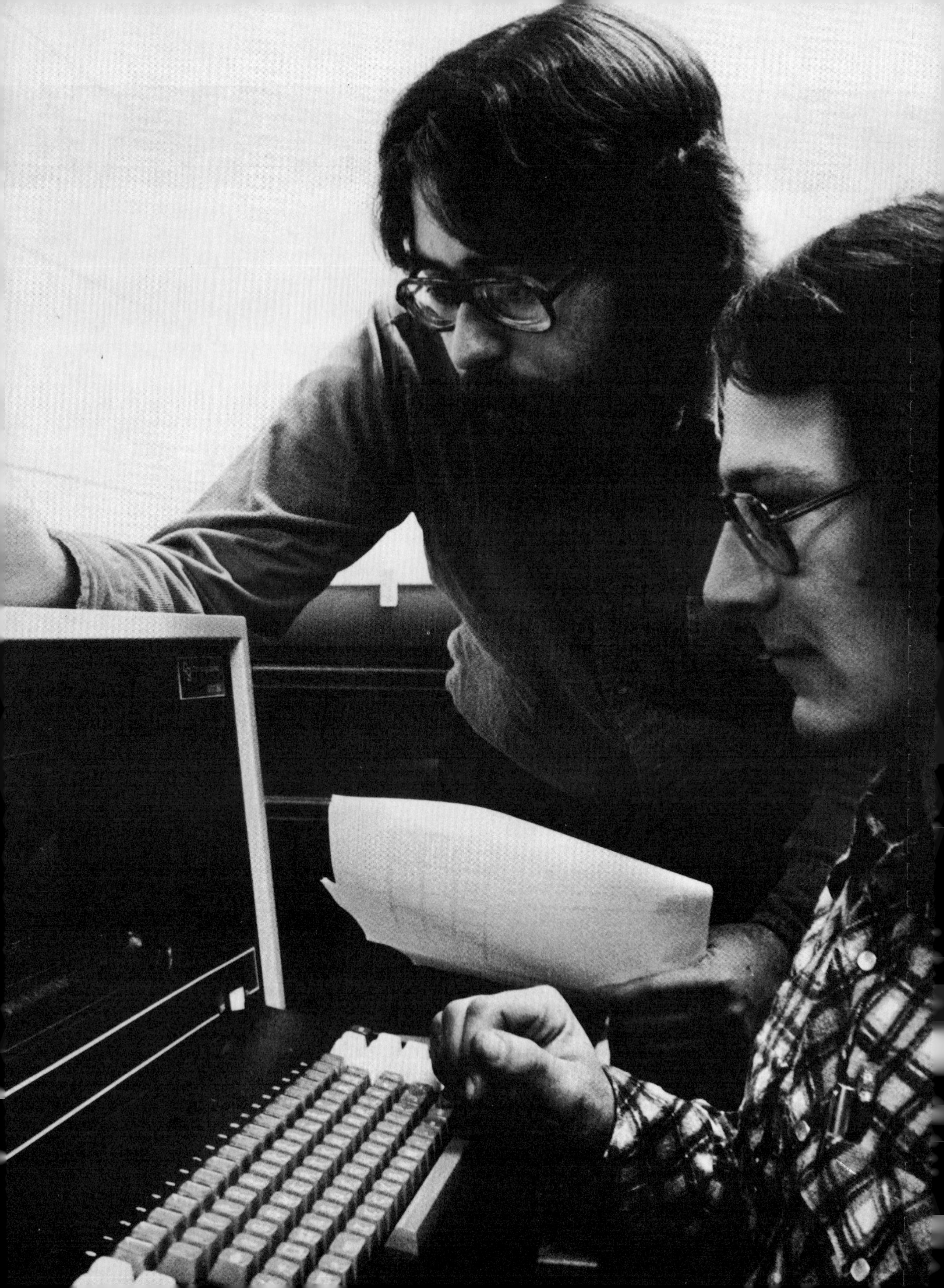

Chapter 8
Handling Wire Copy

In providing readers with news of a non-local origin, newspapers and broadcasting stations use stories sent by one or more of the wire services in the United States such as the Associated Press (AP) or United Press International (UPI). Additionally, news copy may come from foreign news agencies, supplemental feature services such as King Features, and a newspaper's own bureaus. Depending on how many services a particular newspaper has, two or three million words of copy per day could be received. The task of the wire or news editor is to select and edit the wire copy from these sources for each day's edition or newscast.

At the beginning of each AP or UPI news cycle, one for morning news and another for the afternoon, the wire service sends a budget or list of the major stories the service will transmit during that cycle. Of course, many additional late-breaking stories and other material not included in the news budget will be carried, but the budget gives the wire editor some assistance in planning his news schedule for a day.

If each story were complete when received in a news room, it would simplify the wire editor's task, but many times story corrections, new news leads or completely new stories are sent. The first indication of a major news story being sent comes in the form known as a bulletin, which is followed immediately by bulletin adds. Most newspapers will keep available news space open until deadline time for late-developing stories or more information for the continuing story. Sometimes it may take several hours to receive a developing story. When this happens, the service usually sends an entirely revised story after the continuing story is completed. This story will be slugged (headed) "no pickup."

It is important for the wire editor to handle a developing story carefully. The folio and slug (identifying elements) of each section of the story must be preserved. For example, the folio number, s35, indicates that the story was the thirty-fifth item on the state wire. This number will be referred to on any precedes, inserts, or pickups. Because there are many abbreviations and special terms used for wire copy, you need to see the end of this chapter for a definition list for some of the abbreviations and terms.

If the wire editor has a question about a particular story, the editor calls the nearest bureau for information. Editors also must watch wire copy carefully for misspellings, excessive modifiers, and excessive attribution.

LOCALIZE WIRE COPY

Wire copy should be localized when appropriate. Many stories of national importance can be localized by an interview with a local authority. A story about the rising cost of automobiles can be localized through an interview with a local import dealer. An economics professor from a local college could be used to add additional noteworthy perspective to the story. Compare the following wire story with the localized version.

Wire Service Story

American auto prices rose an average of 16 percent last year, a report released today by Congress revealed.

Rep. Thomas Hansen, R-Hawaii, said in Washington today that the 16 percent increase in auto prices had contributed to the nine percent decline in auto sales during the year.

Imported-car prices rose only 3 percent, while import sales were up 20 percent last year.

Localized Story

The rising cost of American-made cars is creating a boom in foreign car sales. One local import dealer says his sales are up 18 percent his year despite a general slow-down in U.S. auto sales. The owner of Import Motors, Robert Smith, says he believes U.S. car prices may double within the next five years.

This confirms a national report released today by Congressman Thomas Hansen of Hawaii. Hansen says American car prices have risen 16 percent with a corresponding decline in sales. In contrast, imports have increased only three percent in price, and foreign car sales are up nearly 20 percent.

WIRE GLOSSARY

ADV. — advance; a story to be used sometime in the future.

AMS, PMS — morning and evening newspapers.

BC — indicates item can be used immediately by either AMS or PMS, designation used on Sunday advances.

BJT — budget; summary or major stories.

BUN — bulletin.

Cycle — Complete news report for either morning or evening papers.

CQ — correct.

Folio — name, date and page number (or any one of these).

FYI — for your information.

HFR — hold for release.

LD or lede — lead.

Pickup — used to designate where story is to begin after a new lead or insert.

No pickup — revised story containing all previous material.

Roundup — usually an undated story involving more than one location for the story. For example, an election return story.

CATEGORY CODES

a and b — domestic, non-Washington news item.

f — news copy designed for financial page.

i — international item.

n — stories of state and regional interest.

q — results of single sports event.

s — sports stories.

v — nationwide news digests, late news advisories.

w — Washington-datelined stories.

Name_____   **Exercise 51**

Directions: The following bulletin came over the wire one hour before an 11 a.m. deadline for the first edition. At 10:30 a.m. more information came over the wire. Edit and write a 1-18-3 headline for your 6-column front page. Make the copy bold face.

s26

BUN

Urgent   zyrzziycss   8-29,dx

an31

DROWN LAKE (AP) — A fifteen year old Drown Lake young lady was found murdered here today. The body was discovered at about 9:30 A.M. on Rippon road about 13 miles Northeast in Collins county.

The girl died of a wound in the skull from a gun according to the police authorities who reported the mruder.

Rippon road, where the girl's body was found was described as only one half mile in length and almost completely without traffic. Residents of this community consider it to be a lover's lane.

-30-

s38

zyrzziyccs   2nd ld.   8-29, dx   an31

Precede Down Lake s26

DROWN LAKE (AP) — A fifteen year old Drown Lake girl, Connie Alexander, was found murdered near here today on Rippon road, about 13 miles northeast of here in Collins county.

pickup 2nd graf s26

Name_____ **Exercise 52**

Directions: By the morning newspaper deadline additional details were available on the Drown Lake murder. Edit the wire copy into one story for the morning edition and write a 4-48-2 headline for an 8-column page.

s56

3rd ld.　　　　　　Precede s38 Drown Lake　　　　qxxzzla　　　　8-27-an31

DROWN LAKE (AP) — The body of Connie Alexander, 15, a Drown Lake High School sophomore, was discovered yesterday on a deserted county road about 13 miles northeast of Central Valley.

She had been shot twice in the head with a small calibre pistol and the wounds caused her death, according to an autopsy report from the Collins county coroner.

Miss Alexander, dauther of Mr. and Mrs. John C. Allexander of Drown Lake, reportedly left home Tusday night to attend a teen dance in the youth activities center here. She apparently was not seen by anybody at the dance, but Police Sgt. Sam G. Gurney fo the local police department said she ahd signed the dance register.

Her body was found by a young people thic mornign on Rippon Road, a short, deserted road which is known as a lovers lane. She was fully clothes byt her hands and face were bloodied. Collins County District Attorney Robert J. Ruth said an autopsy report shoed no indication of sexual assault.

Miss Alexander's father is an employee of the local fire department. The family has lived here about ten years.

-30-

s102

4th ld   Precede s56   Jonesville   qlzzala

8-27   an31

DROWN LAKE (AP) — Attorneys have been appointed for two teenaged youths being questioned about the gunshot slaying of Connie Alexander, 15, of Drown Lake, according to Collins County District Attorney Robert J. Ruth.

The yuuths, one 16 and one 18, were arrested in their nearby homes in Grover early Wednesday morning, after police learned that the girl had been seen with one of them. Ruth said that James Eastland of   Grand Valley had been appointed by Juvenile Judge Mary Driscoll to represent the 16 year old youth.

Atty. Bruce Bullwinkli of Central Valley, was appointed by Judge Clarence G. Hughes to represent the 18 year old in County District Court, if the case should go to court.

"We talked to him at length, and then asked the judge to appoint an attorney," Ruth said. We feldt he should have an attorney even though we're only investigating."

"Nobody's been charged," he said. "They're being held either on suspicion or as material witnesses. There's no question, though, that there ahs been a homicide," Ruth said.

Pickup 1st graf s56

Chapter 9

Dangerous Copy

Copy which may be libelous, in poor taste, or a threat to privacy could be considered "dangerous copy" because if it were published, the reporter, copy editor and newspaper could be in legal trouble.

LIBEL

Beginning editors can easily become confused when confronted with the topic of libel. You may find it easier to ignore questions on this subject or you may censor all suspected libelous material without checking it. With a basic understanding of libel, however, these situations can be avoided.

Libel centers around the principle that everyone has a right to a good reputation as well as legal redress for protection of his or her reputation under civil law. Generally, libel can be defined as a defamation of a person's reputation or business. Any person claiming he or she has been libeled must be able to prove defamation, identification of himself or herself and publication of the defamation. In addition, a person must prove in most states that the reporter, writer or editor failed to exercise reasonable care in preparing the story.

When the defamation is evident (libel per se) from the words or phrases used, it is easy for the reader to interpret or understand the libel. Physicians and lawyers, for example, are considered professional people in any community and any charges of dishonesty, incompetency or stupidity about them could be highly libelous and in poor taste. College teachers also are considered professionals.

A few obvious words and phrases that could injure a person's reputation, if used in a news story include: embezzler, whore, criminal, seducer, crook, unreliable person, unchaste coed, prostitute, swindler, liar, hypocrite, traitor, degenerate, adulterer and abductor. You should avoid using these dangerous words when referring to someone in an article.

The second type of libel refers to hidden defamation (libel per quod). With libel per quod, a story can defame a person while making no name reference to him or her as an individual. Libel per quod involves libel by implication. The words themselves are not libelous, but the overall context of the article is capable of a defamatory meaning. If an article implies that the football coach at the local high school is completely incompetent and stupid without using the coach's name in the article, it still would identify that person to a newspaper's readers and be libelous. The language may not be libelous about the coach, but the implication is.

The publication requirement of libelous material is that it be brought to the attention of a third party who can recognize the defamation.

Contrary to the belief held by many beginning editors and writers, letters-to-the-editor material and guest opinion columns are the responsibility of the news staff, not the guest writers. Citizens irked by the town mayor or police chief frequently send letters to their town newspaper editor in the hope of revenge on the editorial page. An editor's refusal to publish such items may be countered with "I'll take the responsibility for what I've said." Don't believe it. Every person on the newspaper staff, including the backshop people and the boy or girl who delivers the newspapers, theoretically is responsible for everything on its pages.

This also includes libelous quotes. Young reporters often have the idea that any questionable or defamatory material is safe as long as it is attributed to someone else. Regardless of the source, libelous quotes could bring legal trouble if published.

Another element that news editors must avoid is malice. Malice results from the action of a news writer or editor deliberately libeling a person. This happens when a person falsifies material. If public officials or public figures are named or implied, malice then refers to actual malice. Actual malice is defined by the courts as knowledge of falsity or reckless disregard for whether the material is false.

Avoiding malice can be accomplished usually by using fair and accurate reports of any controversial story. The extra effort on the news desk plays the greatest part in catching possible libel in a story. That additional 5 to 10 minutes used to recheck the spelling and accuracy of names, places and circumstances will not only cut down the probability of publishing a libelous article, but will also increase credibility of the newspaper.

The major defenses for libel include the following:

TRUTH. This is the best defense possible, but it is not always usable because of its difficulty to prove. Proof of truth comes mainly from people not connected with the newspaper, because the reporter or another news writer usually does not witness the actual event. Any person or group, on the other hand, has the burden of proving malice intended by the newspaper. In other words, they must show that the newspaper intended to harass the individual or, in some cases, had prior knowledge of the falsehoods and published the story with reckless disregard for the truth.

You also have to be careful about publishing defamatory charges or statements. The article itself may be entirely accurate, but if the paper is not prepared to prove the truth of the charges, then the paper may be without a defense in court. Truth, not accuracy, is a defense in court.

In using truth as a defense, the over-worked concept of objectivity is tested. A news person who fails in getting both sides of a story or checking information thoroughly runs the risk of showing that he or she was indifferent to others' rights and was careless. The copy editor, however, cannot afford this negligence.

No justification exists in court for publishing falsehoods that might delight readers, but show a lack of concern for other people's reputations. Nor does this vindication exclude the column writer who writes about a woman and her personal affairs. The courts tend to be protective of a woman's reputation. These preceding general concepts encompass the entire content of a newspaper, including the letter-to-the-editor section and advertisements.

FAIR COMMENT. Newspapers and individuals in our free society have a right under the First Amendment to comment on public activities of people and institutions affecting the public's interest. Pure expressions of opinion are protected, but those opinions having implied allegations may result in a libel suit.

A food critic, for example, may comment about the meal he or she ate, the service and the atmosphere of the restaurant in his or her review, but that critic cannot generalize beyond his or her dining experience. If a food critic wrote, "It's a little wonder that this restaurant consistently violated health standards," then such a comment would be libelous. It contained an implied allegation about the restaurant.

Entertainment activities such as plays, concerts, political addresses and sporting events may be safely criticized. But, the comments must be fair, have some basis of truth in them and not be written maliciously.

A news writer may editorialize safely that the city's mayor is unsympathetic with minority groups' demands because he has refused many times to discuss them. The news writer may say that the high school team is badly coached this year because the team lacks discipline.

On the other hand, a news writer cannot write on the mayor's personal life without regard for the truth or good intentions. If he or she fails these two tests, then the writer's article could be considered libelous. Speculations that the high school basketball coach is a degenerate or a crook also are defamatory remarks.

PRIVILEGE. Of the three complete defenses, privilege is the most complicated to generalize in a few sentences because what is privileged material in one state may not be in another. It is safe to say that privileged materials can be printed even though they may be false.

Privileged material primarily involves so-called judicial, congressional and presidential records and such proceedings as legislative and city council meetings. Reports of these government events are privileged if they are fair and accurately reported.

Citizens' advisory meetings, student government meetings or other group meetings or activities are not included in this defense, no matter how official they are in a commuity. Avoid publishing any defamatory charges made at such meetings. Otherwise, those libelous remarks may result in a court suit.

FEDERAL CONSTITUTION DEFENSE. This defense basically involves an individual who is either a public official or a public figure. Such an individual in a libel case must prove that the newspaper published the information with the knowledge that it was false or with a reckless disregard for the truth. The constitution defense will protect most stories containing defamatory remarks about a public official or figure's public life or position.

PRIVACY

Two concepts center around privacy. The first deals with a person's right to be let alone and the other one concerns privacy as it relates to governmental secrecy. Generally, most people agree that the privacy of individuals needs protection, but the extent of this coverage has not been fully defined. Almost all lawyers and newsmen favor the concept of privacy for individuals, but not for governmental officials when an activity involves the "public's right to know."

Similarly, individuals lose their right to privacy whenever something puts them in the news because of "the public's right to know." The more important a person becomes in public, the more he or she loses the right to be let alone. For example, if a person is elected mayor of Central Valley, then that person has lost some privacy. But, if that person became governor of the state, he or she would have even less privacy, especially in public life.

While the law of libel protects a person's reputation, the developing law of privacy guards one's personality. A person's privacy may be invaded in four ways.

1) A reporter intrudes upon a person's physical solitude to gather information for a story. Such intrusion could include the reporter trespassing on private property or using a spying device;
2) The publication of private information about a person which is not newsworthy or a part of a public record. This usually involves the publication of private matters or activities violating ordinary decencies;
3) The publication of information which places a person in a false position or "false light" in the public eye; and
4) Some element of a person's personality or name is appropriated for commercial use or gain.

Unlike libel situations, truth is not an absolute defense in an invasion of privacy case, nor is an absence of malice a complete defense. Interpretations of privacy invasion vary so vastly from state to state that it becomes impossible to follow specific guidelines for respecting a citizen's right of privacy.

Thus, in many editing situations, the copy editor must study the state's privacy and libel laws and use good taste and judgment as guides for respecting another's rights. These laws are usually available in the library in the state's code books. If not, copy editors should request their editors to make such volumes available to the city desk.

In the state code books, libel laws are listed under libel or defamation. Privacy laws also may be listed under these headings or under a different section. Ask the librarian who is familiar with your state's code book to help you find the needed laws. Several state press associations have published a compilation of state laws affecting the mass media in their states.

OBSCENITY

Obscenity is one of the most difficult concepts to define. Court interpretations have changed the definition many times in the past 50 years, but today the court requires three tests before a work can be considered obscene:

1. Does the work taken as a whole lack serious literary, artistic, political or scientific value?
2. Would the average person, using contemporary community standards, find the work as a whole appealing to prurient interest (morbid interest in nudity, sex or excretion)?
3. Does work offend community standards of decency as specifically defined in state law?

COPYRIGHT

The Copyright Act of 1976 replaced the outdated 1909 statute to conform to a recognition of the new electronic media. Film, videotape, and photographs may now be copyrighted. Copyright law protects the work for the lifetime of the author/producer plus 50 years. Portions of a work may be used ("fair use" concept), however, as long as it does not impair the market value of the work. Restrictions on "fair use" vary; fair use usually isn't applicable to profit making organizations such as a newspaper.

MISCELLANEOUS

There are many other restrictions that may have some applicability. For example, it is against federal law to publicize a lottery. You may report newsworthy results of a major lottery or a state-operated lottery in your state, but otherwise, you should avoid lotteries. For example, you should not publish a story promoting a local club raffle.

The journalist also faces restrictions that may or may not be legal. If your state has an open meeting and open records law, does it apply to local government? It may take a court case to find out.

Special care should be given in the following cases:

SEX CRIMES: Handle with as much care as possible. State that the crime was committed, provide essential facts, but don't go into detail. For example, you might report a rape case like this:

> A 21-year-old Central Valley woman was raped early this morning as she returned home from work. Police are seeking a 6-foot man, weighing about 175 pounds.

CRIME STORIES: Provide the facts, but don't sensationalize with morbid details. Avoid going into the "how" of the crime. Juvenile names should never be used without the court's permission. Don't report that a person is arrested for questioning. Report suspect's name only when a charge has been filed.

RACE: Unless the race is an important part of the story, it should not be mentioned. If, though, John Smith is the first black mayor of Central Valley, use it. Sometimes in describing fugitives in crime stories, race may be important.

SUICIDE: Don't say someone committed suicide until the coroner has ruled the death a suicide. As in any crime story, state the facts simply without detail. Attribute the suicide ruling to the coroner.

HANDICAPPED: Never joke about a handicap. Don't mention a handicap unless it is essential to the story.

The copy editor in practicing good taste must read each story with some general thoughts in mind such as: 1) Can I justify this item as a news item or merely an item of gossip? 2) Are these items essential to the news story? 3) Am I editing this story for the "public's right to know" or merely because I think it's amusing? 4) Are these items accurate or merely rumor? 5) Are the choice of words lewd or vulgar? 6) Am I hurting an innocent party who may not deserve such treatment?   7) In a story involving a possible invasion of privacy, did the writer have the individual's permission or consent for the information? and 8) In gathering the information, was the reporter on public or private property and did that reporter have a legal right to be there?

These preceding suggestions provide a good starting point from which a beginning copy editor can add other standards of good taste and judgment in editing copy.

These are some ways for editing dangerous copy:

From a news story:

Unedited

The Central Valley School District failed to renew the contract of high school teacher John Lawrence. That decision was made after a discussion of his immoral behavior toward teachers, especially the men.

Edited

The Central Valley School District failed to renew the contract of high school teacher John Lawrence. That decision was made after a discussion of his behavior.

From a sports column:

Unedited

The coach will have a difficult decision to make this year when it comes to choosing the starting team. Most of the players are so dumb that they don't know which way to run with the football — especially Lamle Lamb. Who eliminated the entrance standards to Central Valley for him?

Edited

The coach will have a difficult decision to make this year when it comes to choosing the starting team.

From a news story:

Unedited

The court case of Theordore Backe, of Central Valley, for driving drunk on the old north highway last Thursday evening was delayed this morning until next Wednesday morning at 8:30 a.m. in Municipal Court Jude Tom Yazid took this action. Backe, a Ph.D. who teaches library science at Central Valley Community College was intoxicated when city policeman Grady McNutt stopped his vehicle. McNutt arrested Backe for reckless driving and for driving while intoxicated.

Edited

The case of Theodore Backe, 1611 Cherry Road, for driving while intoxicated on the old north highway last Thursday was delayed today by Municipal Court Judge Tom Yazid until Wednesday at 8:30 a.m. Backe is a library science professor at Central Valley Community College.

Name _____   **Exercise 53**

Directions: You should edit or rewrite any of the following sentences that could lead to a successful libel action against your publication. Then explain why each of the following items would or would not be the basis of a possible libel suit.

a. From a news story:

   Michael York, 450 Country Rd., shot and killed his wife, Marie, while alone with her in their house yesterday. Police arrested York on second-degree murder charges.

b. From a book review in the *Free Press:*

   Dwight Ross's book on the history of Central Valley is far below his usual high standards. It is a terrible book by any criteria. Perhaps if he didn't drink so much now and during the past year, he could get back to his former literary level. Our local author is a disgrace to our town!

c. From a headline in the *Free Press:*

   York found "Not Guilty" in the murder of his wife!

d. From a headline in another paper:

   York found not guilty in the murder of his wife

e. From an editorial:

   Obviously we are not alone in our opinion. Policeman James Foster was fired because of his political beliefs. According to Dwight Smith, Collins County Democratic chairperson, the local Democratic power group felt that Foster was not longer useful to them.

189

f. From a news story:

Mary Sue (Kathy) Snyder, 19, committed suicide today. An empty sleeping pill bottle and a note, which stated "Good-bye," was found beside her. The coroner is investigating her demise.

g. From a speech:

Harry Lewis told some members of a Collins county investigating : committee that Professor James P. Johnson, who teaches political science at the local university, is widely known as a Communist by his students, stated TV Newscaster David Rich.

h. From a trial:

Witness Sally Ethan added, "That man — Tom Holt is the robber, not the defendant." The judge told the jury to disregard the remark.

i. From a letter to the editor:

Football Coach Loyd Hicks was sober at Saturday's game, and wearing a clean shirt.

j. From a syndicated column:

"That earthquake in the State this week didn't do much damage. Many thought it was another of the Governor's quaint remarks."

Directions: Edit and write a 2-30-2 headline for an 8-column format.

LEACH

Bert (linda) Leach, 26, of Central Valley, is believed to be guilty of manslaughter following an accidnet yesterday after her truck collided with a car 30 miles north west of the valley highway. Two Central Valley residents were killed in this accidents.

The victoms, Norman Sagert, 51, and his wife, Arlene, 47, both of 1313 Robertson Drive were killed on impact when their automobile was dragged 200 feet down the highway by the tractor-tractor diven by Ms. Leach.

Also in the Sagert's car were his son, Danny, 17, and a friend, Helen Ruth, 17, of 161 Ashland Street. Danny remains in critical condition at Central Valley Memorial Hospital, and Ruth is there, but she is in fair condition. Both Danny and Ruth are seniors at Central Valley High School.

According to police and witnesses, Ms. Leach said that she was drunk when the accident occured, but that "she was sorry." Ms. Leach also said that she was nervous driving the tractor trailer, and that the Sagert's car seemed to get in her way on the road. As of press time, no formal charges have been brought against Ms. Leach.

Name _____ **Exercise 55**

Directions:

FOOD POISONING

Food poisoning today sent 39 CVU students to the Central Valley Memorial Hospital. Twenty other students were sent there yesterday.

Symptoms seemed to have started yesterday afternoon, but it wasn't until 9:15 last night that students started arriving at the hospital for treatment.

Beverly Knocks, a worker in one of the CVS's cafertia, speculated that the cause of the poisoning may have been an egg and cottage cheese salad severed at lunch or the fish served at dinner or the sausage served at breakfast, all of which she said smelled bad.

According to J. B. Larco, President of CVU, said that "lab tests on samples of yesterday's and today's menues were starting this morning. As of now, we can only speculate that it was food posining. The students, who were admitted to the hospital, have been asked to list everything they ate for the last two days. In this way, we might be able to locate common diets."

Jeff Brown, one of the students who was admitted to the hospital last night, point out that he did not eat in the CVU's cafeteria yesterday, but stated that "I had a hamburger, fires, and a salad at the Pit yesterday noon."

I believe that the food poisoning I had was a result of the PIT's food. Besides, everyone on campus knows that they only reason anyone goes to the PIT is for convenience. The food service is fairly bad; that is, if you order something besides hamburger and fried."

Of the 20 students admitted last night to the hospital, only two remain in the hospital as of press time. All 39 students admitted today are still in the hospital.

Name _____ **Exercise 56**

Directions: Edit, and write a 2-18-2 headline for 5-column tabloid format.

POLICE SUSPENSIONS

Central Valley — Three Central Valley policemen were suspended for 17 days Tue. because of their involvement in an altercation with two Little Rock, Arkansas, men Tuesday of last week.

Acting Police Chief Pat Garrity suspended Seargent John Alire and Patrolmen Randy Bauer and Phil Oates without pay. Alire has been with the police for about 4 years. Bauer and Oats, former New York City officers were hired in January.

Garrity said his action follows an internal investagtion and a hereing August 30. Letters of repremand will be placed in the personal life of each man. The three can appeal the disciplinery action to Central Valley's, personnel director, Ronald Ziegler.

The acting chief said the three officers used poor judgment in chasing down two young men who had thrown a half empty beer bottle in front of there private car in the Saint Vrain Canyon. The officers were offduty, out of uniform and out of there own jursidiction at the time.

Name_____ **Exercise 57**

Directions: Edit the following DAILY RECORD for a 14-pica boxed standing column.

Central Valley Memorial Hospital Admitted:

Rob Wagner, 688 Remington

Mrs. Kathy Synder, Aggie Village, Apt. 34B.

Central Valley Memorial Hospital Dismissed:

Frank Valdez, 1819 W. Mulberry

Births: no one.

Accidents:

　　6:30 a.m., Thursday, Earl Callaway, 1026, reported theft of two hundred and fifty dollars of recording tapes from his house. Officer McNutt said that he could not estimate the loss.

8:55, Thursday, Rev. Mark M. Burke, reported the theft of a widnow, six screens from a home under construction.

　　Officer McNutt ested the loss at $80.

1:20, Thursday, Dave Bloom, 1095 Luke, reported the theft of gas from his car.

5:40, Thursday, Lybel Elbel, a florist, reported two stolen tackel boxes containing tackle and other fishing items.

Officer McNutt estimed the loss at $65, and reported no suspects.

10:20 p.m., Thursday, Don Eyers, 632 Stover, reported a spare tire and wheel missing from his new pickup truck.

Ofcicer McNutt estimed the loss at $85, and reported no suspects.

11:10 p.m., Thursday, Julian Caster, an employee at the Pizza Factory, was allegedly struck by Susan Davis, 4 alcott, She is twenty-years-old.

　　According to a police report, Davis and some girl friends were acting disorderly and shouting vagular words at other customers. They then left without paying the bill, police said.

###

Name _____ Exercise 58

Directions: Edit and write a 2-36-1 headline for a 6-column newspaper.

TRANSCRIPTS

In an unusual move, the entire 1600 page transcript of testimony taken by the Central Valley Grand Jurey in their investigation of the death of Fred Noyes has been made public.

Judge Charles Never of Central Valley District Court ordered the release of the transcripts Thurs.

The release was requested by Cenvral Valley dist. attorney Cedric Hardmen. who presented the document for City Manager Norm Feirt and city council members.

Feit made the presentation at the major's office Thrusday afternoon, shortly after the jurey returned a critical report, but not inditements, as a result of Noyse"s death.

The transcrip, which can be read in city council chambers in the city and county building, are believed to have been made public for revew for person's who may be critical of the jury's decision.

Some Central Valley residents have stated a Central Valley police officer and perhaps some sherif's deputies should have been indicted for abust of Noyse.

State law permits the re-lease of such transcripts when a jury probe results in an indic tment.

However a judge must order such a release when no indictments are amade. Usuly their is no such order.

###

Name _____ **Exercise 59**

Directions: Edit and write a 1-18-2 headline for a 5-column paper.

KERR

CENTRAL VALLEY — A former supertendent of Florida Pioneer home in Greenville Friday pleaded innocent to eleven counts of embezzlement at his arrignment in Collins County district court here.

District Judge Ewing Kerr set a November 15 trial date for Matt Lopez, the supertendent

Lopez's attorney siad after the hearing that he planned to file a motion to ddismis all charges. the attorny claimed Lopez was denied his constitutional rights at a pre-liminary hearing earlier in Central Valley justice court.

The charges against Lopez were filled after a examination of records of the state retirement home turned up alledged discrepeencies in the funds expened.

The audit was contucted by the state auditors office, and it's findings caused the State Bord of Charities and Reform to dismis Lopez in early April.

Lopez originally was charged with nineteen counts of embezzlement for aledgedly using 6,922 dollars of state and trust fund money to buy items for himself, friends and family members. 8 charges later were dismised in justice court.

###

Name_____   **Exercise 60**

Directions: Edit and write a 1-14-2 headline for an 8-column format.

CLIMBING ACCIDENT

Two men were killed yesterday in a rock climing accident in Palmer Park west of here. According to the police, the d4ead victims are Ned Halpin, 1305 Kirkwood, and Jimmie Catlin, 516 Fort Road.

Officers said that the two men probably were pushed from a 40-foot cliff in the Park. Hslpin was killed instantly and Catlin died several hours later at Central Valley Memorial Hospital of head and internal injuries.

Doctors said they believe they head Catlin mumble "Glass" as he drifted in and out of conscousness before his death.

Pro football star Chip Glass, 213 Thunderbird, was arrested and incarcerated in the Collins County Jail for questioning.

###

Name_____ **Exercise 61**

Directions: Edit and write a 2-30-1 headline for an 8-column format.

JAIL ESCAPE

Police officers and a cemetery caretaker were the objects of assault and abduction yesterday when three men, all awaiting trial on other charges, escaped from the Collins County Jail.

The scenario began when Matt Lopez, of 726 Cherry, Ralphie Owen, 371 Sherwood, and Steve Walker, 1188 Westwood escaped from the Collins County Jail.

Later, the men were arrested in Central Valley.

According to police, the crminals are suspected of assulting, robbing and abducting Chester Johnson, 76, a cemetery worker who was working near the jail, and forcing him to accompany them to Central Valley in his vehicle.

Two of the suspects got out near downtown Central Valley, according to Johnson, but the third didn't get out until near the city limits. Police said that Owen was apprehended at exactly 9:16 Saturday d evening at 32nd aveenue and First Street and Walker was nabbed an hour later at the Airport Motor Inn. Walker approache an offduty policeman with a corwbar and that led to his arrest.

Lopex, meanwhile, is thought to be the driver of a car which almost killed Patrolmen Frank Videz, who tried to stop it because it was reported stolen and involved in a hit-run accident. He was jailed for investigation of vehicular assault and escape.

Lopez, Walker and Owens are allegedly guilty of armed robbed and carrying concealed weapons in non-related incidents, and were awaiting trail on these charges.

Name_____ **Exercise 62**

Directions: Edit the story; put a 2-30-2 head on it for a 6-column paper.

BOSS — Second Day Story

An 18 year old suspect, who was charged this afternoon with arson, is being questioned by Central Valley police concerning a $780,000 fire which swept throu gh a Central Valley toy factory yesterday afternoon around 4 p.m. and caused the death of an employee.

Robert K. Boss, an unemployed high school dropout and a local resident of Central Valley was charged with arson after being arrested at noon today at his home near Central Valley toy plant.

He was seen fleeing the scene of the fire, Youth Products, Inc., 1316 Adams Lane, shortly after 4 o'clock, when the fire broke out and spread throughout the entire building.

His mother confirmed to police that Boss was not at home at the time of the fire, but said that he was home later in the evening.

The four alarm fire, which took 3 hours and 10 minutes to bring under control by firemen and substitute firemen, caused extensive damage to the plastic products firm.

The fire was spotted at 4 p.m. bya passing Sunday motorist who also saw Boss running from the factory without his coat.

James W. Dary, 21-1/2, of 214 South Bend Ave., Apt. 216, an employee of the firm, was found dead of asphyxiation in a washroom of the plant.

Dary had been drinking at a local bar with a friend and decided to sleep in the washroom until his 11 p.m. shift becan.

Firemen and other officials determined that gasoline was used to start the fire. The firm employees 180 workers.

compugraphic videosetter universal
INPUT SWITCHES ON UNIVERSAL MUST BE IN
THE EXTERNAL AND JUSTIFY POSITIONS

Chapter 10

Typography

By Jean Lundberg*

A prerequisite to effective newspaper and magazine design is an adequate understanding of typography. An editor who wants the audience to read more of what has been written must learn to use type effectively.

Typography refers quite simply to the design and appearance of typefaces themselves or more broadly to the total style, arrangement and appearance of printed matter. Since words set in type and then arranged on a page with other elements form the basis of most publications, it should be obvious that typography, however defined, is an important consideration for the editor.

This chapter will introduce typography as the study of typefaces themselves; the chapter on Makeup and Design will address typography in its broader definitions.

As a first step toward learning to use type effectively, the beginner should examine the resemblances and differences among typefaces. Stop reading words for what they say and start looking at the letters that form those words. What do they look like? Are they ornamented or simple? Formal or informal? Of even or varied thickness? Slanted or straight? It won't take long to decide that there must be thousands of variations.

There are. To learn the names of all those types certainly would be a ponderous task. Of those thousands of typefaces, however, only 100 or so are in common use, and a given publication will use only a handful of those. With a little practice, even a beginner can learn to recognize a publication's worth of typefaces.

But what about the rest? Just as it is possible to provide partial identification of a person whose name is unknown by describing his physical characteristics, so is it possible to partly identify a typeface by describing its physical characteristics. All that is needed is a common set of terminology.

---

*Jean Lundberg is an assistant professor of journalism at Colorado State University. She teaches editing and graphics.

RACES OF TYPE

Every person in the world can be classified in terms of his race; so, too, can every typeface. And just as scholars reach somewhat different conclusions about the number of clearly defined races of people in the whole of humanity, so, too, do typographers differ somewhat on the number of races into which to divide the aggregate of types.

One common and easy-to-learn classification scheme divides typefaces into five races: Text, Roman, Gothic, Script and Cursive and Novelty.

Text, sometimes referred to as Old English or black letter, is the oldest of the races, since the movable type first cast by Gutenberg would be classified as a Text. Inspired by the black-letter calligraphy of medieval Germany, the Text types are characterized by heavy vertical strokes and abrupt, angular curves. Some have hairline ornamentation added to the basic letterform.

The Roman race is nearly as old as the Text, since among its members are the types designed and cast by the early Italian printers. While the black-letter style of calligraphy dominated medieval Germany and Northern Europe, white letter, a lighter, more readable style developed at the request of the Emperor Charlemagne, was more common in Italy.

White letter, and the Roman race of types it inspired, has two basic characteristics. In order to be classified as a Roman, a typeface must exhibit both. (1) The letters have serifs — ornamentations at the beginnings and endings of the strokes that form the actual letter. (2) The strokes that form the actual letter are of varying thickness, thinner in the horizontal areas and thicker in the verticals.

The Gothic types are those patterned after the simpler-still letterforms of the ancient Greeks. Inspired by the Industrial Revolution, the Gothics were popular through the mid-1800s, fell out of use during the revivalist Victorian period, and then were rediscovered and popularized after World War I, notably by functional design advocates in Germany.

The Gothic types also have two fundamental characteristics. (1) They are simple and unornamented, the skeletons of letters. (2) The strokes that form the letters are monotonous — that is, all of the same thickness.

The members of the Script and Cursive race all resemble modern handwriting. Their letterforms are informal and slanted to the right.

Novelty is a race of type that might more accurately be described as "Other." Unlike those belonging to the other four races, Novelty types share no common characteristics. They are the misfits, the typefaces that do not belong to any other races.

SUBDIVISIONS

As with people, then, the race is the broadest description of a typeface's physical characteristics and origin. But finer distinctions are possible. To continue the analogy, people from several different countries can all belong to the same race. So, too, can typefaces belonging to different subdivisions all be members of the same race.

Three of the races of type have such subdivisions: Roman, Gothic and Script and Cursive.

A Roman type can be classified in one of three subdivisions according to the shape of its serifs, particularly those at the bottoms of letters, and the extent to which its stroke thicknesses vary.

Oldstyle Roman types have thickly bracketed, wedge-shaped serifs that often appear pointed and minimal thick/thin contrast.

Modern Romans, on the other extreme, have straight, hairline serifs with little or no bracket and maximum contrast between the thick and thin areas of the letters; the serifs are the same thickness as the thin letter areas.

As their name implies, the Mixed (or Transitional) Romans have serifs and thickness contrasts that fall somewhere in between. Indeed, the first Mixed Roman was an effort to improve the legibility of an Oldstyle by increasing the contrast, but without going to the severe, mechanical-looking extreme of a Modern. A Mixed Roman's serifs are bracketed, but not as heavily as an Oldstyle's; they may appear as an Oldstyle serif with the pointed end chopped off. There is marked thick/thin contrast in the strokes of a Mixed Roman, but not as much as in a Modern. Perhaps a more functional title for the Mixed Roman subdivision would be "Other."

Gothic types belong to one of two subdivisions depending on whether their letters have serifs.

The Sans Serif Gothic is the more common, the classic, simple, skeleton of a letter — no serifs, no noticeable thick/thin variation.

The Square (or Slab) Serif Gothic is exactly as it sounds — a Gothic with square-shaped serifs added. The serifs are the same thickness as the letterform itself and show no signs of bracketing.

The Script and Cursive race also has two subdivisions, the distinction made by whether the letters appear joined.

A typeface belongs to the Script subdivision if the majority of the letters are designed in such a way that they appear joined when a word is set in that type. A Cursive typeface has the same informal letterforms, but the letters do not appear to be joined when a word is set.

FAMILIES

"My, but you resemble your father! I could tell you are a Peterson without even asking."

People who are members of the same family often have many of the same general physical characteristics — bone structure, shape of face, hair color and so on. Typefaces that are members of the same family also have common physical characteristics — shape of letter, shape of serif, height of ascender and descender and so on.

A human family is known by the family name of the father; a type family is known by the name given to it by its designer, often the same as his human family name.

Meet some well-known type families:

Caslon, an Oldstyle Roman, was introduced in the early 1700s by William Caslon, an English engraver. The old printer's rule "When in doubt, use Caslon" perhaps accounts for its continuing popularity. Caslon is characterized by its rather tall x-height, the large enclosed area of the lowercase "e" and the nick out of the top of the uppercase "A."

Garamond, designed by Claude Garamond in the early 1500s, is another popular Oldstyle Roman. Garamond and Caslon may well be first cousins, their designs are so similar. Compare the x-heights, the lowercase "e's," the uppercase "A's" and "T's."

Goudy, another Oldstyle Roman, was introduced in 1910 by an American type designer, Frederick Goudy. The diamond-shaped dot on the lowercase "i" makes Goudy easy to identify. Also, the serifs appear to be slightly concave, and there are no perfectly straight or parallel lines in the letterforms.

Bodoni, the most common of the Modern Roman typefaces, was developed about the time of the American Revolution by Giambattista Bodoni, an Italian printer. The classic Modern Roman, Bodoni types are characterized by perfectly straight, thin bottom serifs and the great contrast between thick and thin letter areas.

Cheltenham, a Mixed Roman, was developed in 1904 by Bertram Goodhue, an architect, and remains popular as a newspaper headline face. Cheltenham is one Roman type that exhibits fairly little contrast between thick and thin areas. The right stroke of the uppercase "A" extends over the top of the left; the uppercase "G" has a noticeable beard or chin; the descender of the lowercase "g" is not closed.

Baskerville, Caledonia and *Century* are more typical of Mixed Roman design — simple, easy-to-read crosses between Oldstyle and Modern. All three are popular for both headlines and body type.

Futura and *Kabel* (also known as Cable and Sans Serif) are both popular Sans Serif Gothic types designed by Germans in the 1920s. More recent Sans Serifs that have become popular publication faces include *Helvetica* (Helios is a near-twin.), *Avant Garde* and *Univers*.

The overall monotonous appearance of Univers and its lack of serifs make it a Sans Serif Gothic even though its letterforms do have some thick/thin contrast. That contrast makes Univers easy to identify.

The others are somewhat more difficult to distinguish. The lowercase "a" is one good identifying letter. Futura and Avant Gard both use the "a" that is essentially an "o" with a vertical stroke on the right; Kabel and Helvetica both use the version that resembles a short, upside-down "q." The lowercase "g" is another one to study. Futura, Avant Garde and Helvetica all use the form that resembles an "a" with a tail; Kabel and its derivatives use the more formal combination of two "o's."

Other characteristics to study include the degree to which the letters are round or oval, whether the crossbar on the lowercase "e" is straight or slanted, whether the left and right strokes of the uppercase "M" and "W" is straight or slanted.

Stymie, introduced by American Type Founders in 1931, is perhaps the most widely used of the Square Serif Gothics. The hockey-stick shape of the lowercase "y's" descender and the square dot on the lowercase "i" are good identifying characteristics.

Brush and *Commercial* are common script typefaces; Brush is lighter in weight than Commercial. *Coronet* is a classic example of a Cursive type.

Hundreds of typefaces belong to the Novelty race, many with such interesting names as *Shatter, Broadway, Neon* — even *Gorilla. American Typewriter* is an extremely popular Novelty type.

FAMILY MEMBERS

While members of the same human family share some physical characteristics, they often differ in others. The sons may be taller and thinner than the father; one brother may be heavier than the other; one sister may have more pronounced features than another. Members of the same typeface family differ in similar ways.

Nearly all Roman and Gothic families have members that differ by stance, which refers to whether the letters stand upright or are slanted to the right. For the sake of clarity, the upright members should be called simply "upright." Some printers and typographers, however, refer to them as "roman." The slanted versions are labeled "italic."

Type family members also may vary by weight, or thickness of the letter strokes. The designations "extra light," "light," "book," "medium," "demibold," "bold," and "extra bold" are used to make weight distinctions.

Variations in the widths of letters also may occur. The tall, thin version is "extra condensed" or "condensed; the short, squat version is "expanded" or "extended."

Some typefaces even have "solid" and "outline" versions.

To further complicate the matter, all of these distinctions can occur in combination. For instance, a type may be "italic bold condensed" or "italic light expanded."

A final note: When trying to classify a typeface according to this scheme, begin with the broad characteristics and move to the narrower. Determine race, then, subdivision, then family and, finally, family member. That way, you won't be fooled by a Mixed Roman (which can resemble a Square Serif Gothic) or an italic Roman (which can resemble a Cursive).

1. Text
2. Roman
    2a. Oldstyle
    2b. **Modern**
    2c. Mixed
3. Gothic
    3a. Sans Serif
    3b. Square Serif
4. **Script and Cursive**
    4a. Script
    4b. *Cursive*
5. **Novelty**

Caslon   A T e
Andover   A T e
Goudy Bold   A T E i '
Bodoni   A T E O e m
Times Modern   A T G e g
Times Roman   A T e m

News Gothic   A T M W a e g
Serif Gothic   A T M W a e g
Megaron   A T M W a e g
Avant Garde   A T M W a e g
Universe   A T M W a e g
Stymie   A T a e i y
Studio
Commercial Script
Korinna Kursive
Megaron Light Italic
Megaron Medium Italic
Megaron Bold Italic
Megaron Light
Megaron Medium
Megaron Bold
Megaron Extra Bold
Megaron Medium Condensed
Megaron Bold Condensed
Megaron Extra Bold Condensed

TYPE SIZE

Size of type is measured in points. As indicated in Chapter 4, a point is 1/72 of an inch and is used in vertical measurement of type. Standard type sizes used in the newspaper include 6-point type, often called agate type which is used in box scores and tabulations; 8, 10, 12-point type, often called body type, which is used in the text; and 14, 18, 24, 30, 36, 42, 48, 54, 60, 72, and 84-point type, which is headline or display type.

Measure type from the top of the highest letter (ascender line) to the bottom of the letter going farthest down (descender line).

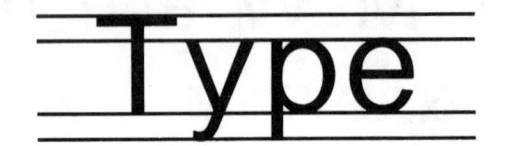

TYPE SELECTION

The principal rule in selection of a type style is to select that type which is most unobtrusive (i.e. does not call attention to itself). Good typography is an aid to the reader; therefore, if the reader is distracted by the type, poor judgment has been used by the editor in type selection.

In selecting type, the editor should remember to use strong contrast in varying headline type. For example, a lightface headline may be contrasted with an extra bold one, or an italic headline may be used with a Roman one near it. However, too many different typefaces or sizes on one page should be avoided or the result will be a cluttered page. Most publications use no more than one type family.

An editor and graphics composer check the type on a page. (Photo by the Temple Daily Telegram.)

Name_____   **Exercise 63**

Directions: Identify the following types by race, subdivision, family and family member.

1. **The Graphic Arts Serve Mankind**

2. The Graphic Arts Serve Mankind

3. *The Graphic Arts Serve Mankind*

4. The Graphic Arts Serve Mankind

5. The Graphic Arts Serve Mankind

6. *The Graphic Arts Serve Mankind*

7. The Graphic Arts Serve Mankind

217

Name_____   **Exercise 64**

Directions: Use available newspapers or magazines to cut and paste examples requested in this exercise.

1. Find one example of each of the following:

    Text

    Oldstyle Roman

    Modern Roman

    Mixed Roman

    Sans Serif Gothic

    Square Serif Gothic

    Script

    Cursive

2. Find examples of the upright and italic stances of the same family.

3. Find examples of at least two different weights of the same family.

4. Find examples of condensed and expanded type.

5. Find examples of three different Novelty types. Use the terminology of the races to describe their characteristics.

6. Find an example of poor type selection for a headline. Explain why you think it is a poor selection.

###

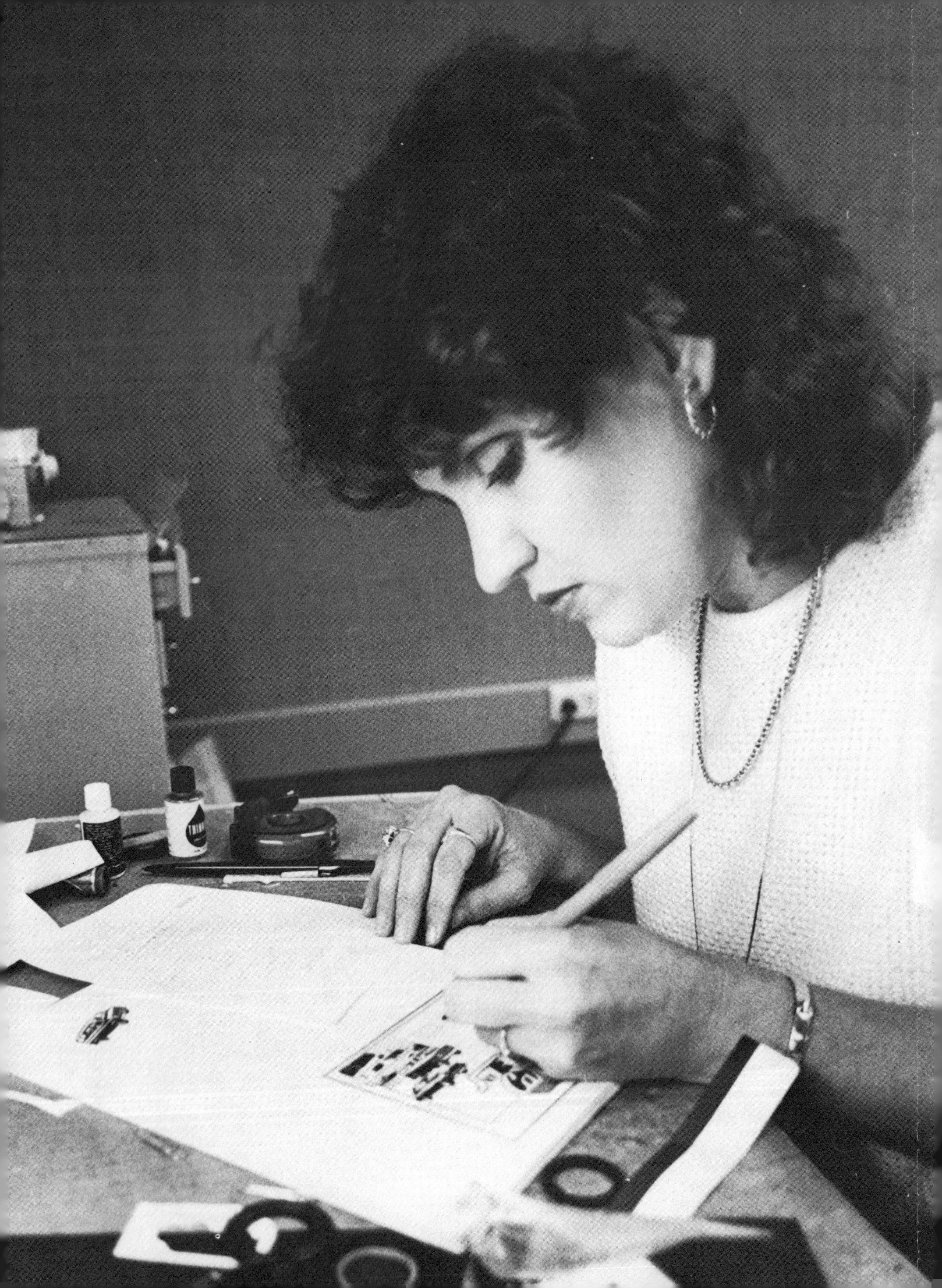

Chapter **11**

Graphics

By Jean Lundberg*

GRAPHICS

Typography, as noted in an earlier chapter, refers not only to the design of typefaces themselves, but also to the total style, arrangement and appearance of printed matter. Graphic design is another term often used to refer to that same, more broad definition of "typography."

Whichever term is used, the importance of effective use of type and effective arrangement of type and other elements should be obvious to the editing student. After all, the editor wants his audience to read and understand the information contained in his publication, and he understands that poor presentation can ruin even the best of copy. (On the other hand, however, he also realizes that good presentation will only call attention to bad copy!)

To be effective, an arrangement of type and other elements must be functional — that is, it must work, it must enhance the communication process. And, in order for such an arrangement to be functional, it must be both legible and logical.

A knowledge of eye movement will help ensure both legibility and logic. First, understand that in Western cultures the human eye more or less naturally moves from left to right and top to bottom. Similarly, it resists moving in opposite directions — right to left or bottom to top. The only exception is a willingness to return to the axis of orientation, the left edge of consecutive lines of type. Second, people read by recognizing the shapes of entire words, not individual letters. And, third, reading is easiest if the eyes can take in a line of words in one easy glance.

With that knowledge, it is possible to develop some guidelines to help ensure that type will be easy to read.

1. Because people read by recognizing the shapes of words, cap-and-lowercase style is easier to read that all-caps, where each word ends up being a rectangle.
2. In addition, because of their complex designs, Text, Script, Cursive and many Novelty types should never be used in all-caps.

---

*Jean Lundberg is an assistant professor of journalism at Colorado State University. She teaches editing and graphics.

3. Arranging the letters of a word from top to bottom, one on top of another, is a poor idea.
4. In order to facilitate reading a line of type in one easy glance, a line ought to have between 39 and 52 characters. Research has shown that 26 characters on a line is the minimum for easy reading, while 52 is the maximum. The so-called optimum is half-way between, 39 characters. Those figures are geared toward an audience of average education; scholars can handle up to 78 characters on a line.
5. Because of the axis-of-orientation phenomenon, flush left and fully justified lines of type are easier to read than those set flush right.

In addition to guidelines based on eye movements, there are three other guidelines based on the size and shape of letters.

1. Research has confirmed the old gut feeling that types with serifs are generally easier to read than those without, particularly for long passage of body type.
2. 8-point type is about the minimum for newspapers and 10-point the maximum; 9-point is most common. Magazines and books should be set no smaller than 10-point. Also consider such other factors as age and reading ability of the audience before determining a body-type size; 10-point would be a poor choice for a children's book.
3. Leading is based on the point size and the x-height of the type selected. 8-point and smaller need 1-point of leading; 10-point and larger need 2-points. These amounts can be decreased if the type has a short x-height (long ascenders and descenders) or increased if it has a tall x-height (short ascenders and descenders). 9-point is a no-man's-land; base the leading on the x-height of the type.

All of these legibility guidelines assume that black type is to be printed on white paper. If that is not the case, if there is to be less contrast between the color of the background and the color of the type (white type on a black background, or blue type on a blue background, for instance), some adjustments are in order. To compensate for a loss of contrast, use a larger type, a bolder type or a simpler type (an Oldstyle Roman or Gothic instead of the thin-seriffed Modern Roman).

In addition to being legible and easy to read, an arrangement of type and other elements must also be logical in order to be functional. Everything from the type selection through the positioning of elements must make sense to the reader. Logic in design is achieved through integration and simplicity.

Integration in design refers to both the aesthetic and the physical. To achieve aesthetic integration, select both a type style and a design scheme that match the content and tone of the article, advertisement, publication or whatever. For instance, a Text type would be appropriate for a headline on an article about early German printers or for the label on a vintage wine, but not so appropriate for a headline on an article about computers or for the label on a new, caffeine-free, sugar-free soft drink. A design scheme based on centering would be appropriate for an invitation to a formal wedding but not for one to a street-corner break dance contest.

Physical integration refers to the simple notion that related elements ought to be located near to one another — headlines near their stories, captions near the illustrations they explain and so on. Physical integration can be achieved through simple propinquity, placing related elements near to one another, or alignment, lining up related elements, preferably on a vertical axis. (Remember, people read from top to bottom.)

If a layout is physically well-integrated, it will automatically exhibit another characteristic of logical design: All of the white space, with the exceptions of planned gutters and leading, will fall to the outside, or perimeter, of the elements. White space trapped in the middle of a layout creates an illogical separation of elements.

Another device to look for in a logical, well-integrated design is the presence of a strong, planned focal point. Every layout, however poorly conceived, will have a focal point, a spot where a reader looks first. The idea of a strong, planned focal point is to let one element so dominate the layout that the reader has no choice but to look there first. A layout with many similar-sized elements competing for attention will confuse the reader.

If a layout has a strong, planned focal point and white space to the outside of the elements, chances are it will also show informal balance, which is another hallmark of functional design. Unless concerns for aesthetic integration demand it, centering and other forms of formal balance should be avoided.

A simple solution to a design problem is often the best solution. A simple layout stands a greater chance of being logical, and it has the added benefit of being easier and less costly to produce.

This notion of simplicity also plays a role in type selection. Strive to keep the number of different styles of type in a given layout to a minimum. When combining types, particularly headline types, select types that clearly contrast or harmonize. Types have adequate contrast if they belong to different races; types that harmonize are those that belong to the same family. For example, a Text type contrasts with any Roman, regardless of subdivision; Bodoni, Bondoni Bold and Bodoni Bold Italic harmonize because they all belong to the same family. Bodoni, a Modern Roman, and Garamond, an Oldstyle Roman, neither harmonize nor contrast; such a combination could be described as a "near miss."

Simplicity also ought to be a consideration in selecting type sizes. Make sure that the differences are enough to be obvious and that they make sense. No one but a printer or designer can readily tell the difference between 12- and 14-point type!

The earth revolves around one axis that lends it structure; so should the simple, logical page design. The edges of every element create lines of force that are called axes. The idea is to have elements share those lines or axes so that they form a kind of backbone for the entire layout. If alignment of elements is used as an integration device, these shared axes will occur naturally. A typical page should have no more than two or so horizontal axes and another two or so vertical axes.

The use of color should also be considered in light of the desires for simplicity and logic. Remember, each additional color requires an additional printing plate and all its associated costs. Color that does not clearly make sense only adds unnecessary complication and cost. For instance, printing a word in red certainly will emphasize it; but the same emphasis could be achieved with a larger size, a contrasting typeface or some other device — all at a considerably lower price.

Simplicity of design also requires simplicity of editorial concept. The good designer will work with writers and editors to establish a single, main theme for the content and then use that main theme as the basis for his design.

Finally, these guidelines for achieving legible, logical, functional design ought to be interpreted as just that — guidelines, not rules carved in stone. There are many instances where the guidelines may conflict, an aesthetic desire for a Sans Serif Gothic body type pitted against the better legibility of a Roman, for instance. In such a case, the designer obviously must make a choice. The point of these guidelines is to help the designer make that decision, and any necessary compensations, based on thought and knowledge rather than whim.

Layout must follow the makeup designed. (Photo by Longmont Times Call.)

Name_____ **Exercise 65**

Directions: Use newspapers, magazines or other publications to locate examples of the following:

1. A headline set in all-caps Text, Script, Cursive or Novelty

2. A word or words with the letters arranged from bottom to top rather than left to right

3. Type set flush left, fully justified and flush right.

4. Type that exceeds the recommended number of characters on a line.

5. Type that is difficult to read because of a lack of contrast between the type and the background on which it is printed.

6. An instance where the designer compensated for a lack of contrast with the background by using larger, bolder or simpler type.

7. Type whose look and style is appropriate for the content and tone of the article or product.

8. Elements that are integrated through alignment.

9. A layout with trapped white space.

10. A layout with a weak focal point.

11. A layout with a strong, planned focal point.

12. A layout that used too many different type styles and/or sizes.

13. A layout with illogical or unnecessary use of color.

14. A layout with effective use of color.

15. A layout that develops a single, main theme.

Directions: Explain and justify each of your selections.

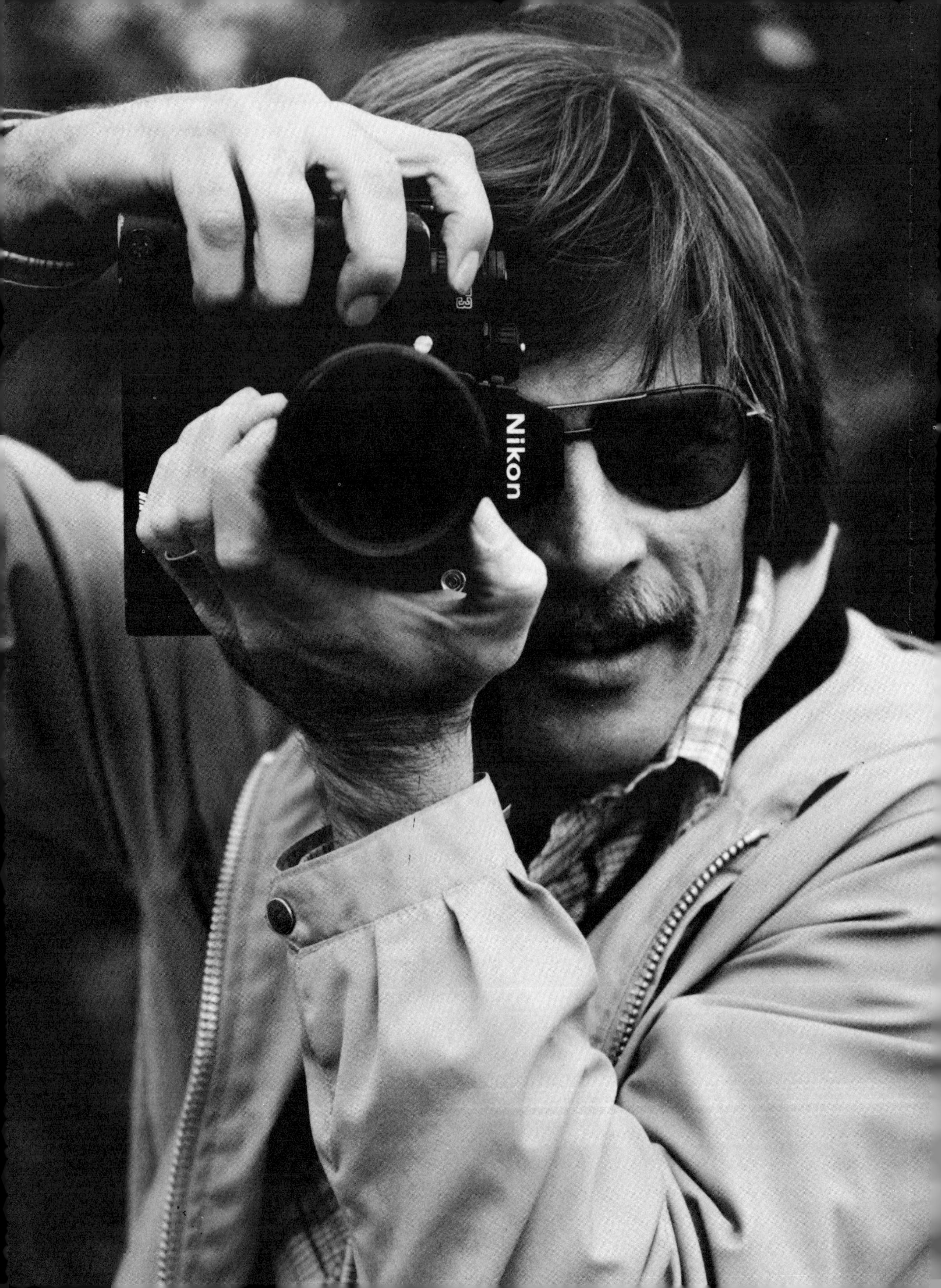
Nikon

Chapter 12
Photo Editing

Most large newspapers have a photo editor, but on smaller ones, the copy editor has the double job of being a part-time photo editor. In either situation, the editor must make the same selection about a photograph that is made about a news story. The editor asks when does a story need a photograph or when could a photograph replace a news story? Today's editor is selecting fewer pictures but giving those chosen more space.

In selecting photographs, you should look for those that will have an immediate impact on the viewers. Obviously, those head-and-shoulder types (often called "mug shots") will not have the same appeal as photographs that deliver a message. Proximity plays an important part in the selection of news stories, but it is not that important for photo selection. Any photograph with human interest appeal can be as interesting to readers in your town as it is to readers in the area where the photograph originated. No publication can afford to offend its readers with photographs that distort or mislead readers. Each photograph you select must be carefully evaluated for wrong impressions, possible libel, and invasion of privacy. Photographs, more than news stories, have a greater potential for these violations.

After you have selected a vertical or horizontal photograph, you can find the interest point of it by moving two L-shaped pieces of cardboard or two rulers over the photograph until you find a chief point of interest. Next, you have to determine what width and depth of the photograph will fit your page layout. Some areas of the photograph usually need to be eliminated (cropped) to add impact to this main point. For example, when the main interest of your photograph is width as in a horizontal one, then the critical proportion to find is the length or depth of the photograph. By using the proportion disk (wheel), the mathematical proportion method, or the diagonal method, you can determine the exact depth or width needed.

To use any of these methods all you need to know is the desired width or depth of the photograph. For example, if you have a cropped vertical photograph that was 10" wide by 8" deep and wanted to run it in two columns wide for your newspaper (and the two columns were a total of 5" wide), any of these methods would tell you how much space you should allow for the depth of the photo when printed as a cut in your newspaper.

Here are the three methods you can use:
(1) Proportion Disk — The proportion disk is made of two pieces of cardboard or plastic with the smaller disk fastened over the larger one. The smaller is movable, allowing any

number shown on either disk to have direct alignment with the other in order to show the desired proportions. To use the proportion disk, you first adjust the width size of the photograph on the smaller disk with the desired width size on the larger disk. Then, you look at the desired space number on the large disk after you have aligned it with that disk number. You next have the exact numerical depth for your photograph.

(2) Mathematical Formula — For this method you use the following formula:

$$\frac{W}{D} = \frac{w}{d}$$ where: W = cropped width of the photo
D = cropped depth of the photo
w = desired width of the cut
d = desired depth of the cut

With this formula, you can always find the value of one side if you know the other three values. Therefore, in the example of a 10″ by 8″ photo, which must be reduced to 5″ width, the formula would work as follows:

$$\left(\frac{W}{D} = \frac{w}{d}\right) = \left(\frac{10}{8} = \frac{5}{d}\right) = (10d = 40) \qquad d = 4''$$
$$\text{cross-multiply}$$

After cross-multiplying these figures to find the missing "d" values in the formula, the answer for the desired depth is four inches.

(3) Diagonal Method — To use this method draw a rectangle of exact width and depth of the cropped photograph. Next, draw a diagonal line from the upper left corner to the lower right one (extend this line if you are enlarging). Starting from the upper left-hand corner, you first measure the desired width, and then draw a perpendicular line from that point until it intersects the diagonal. Then, measure the length of the perpendicular line, which will give you the desired depth of the photograph. If you know the desired depth, you can figure the width by reversing this process:

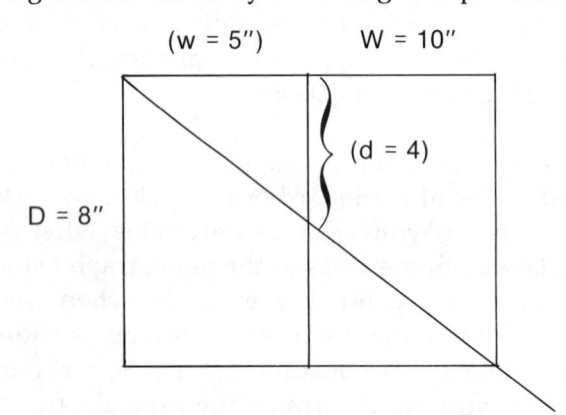

(w = 5″)   W = 10″

} (d = 4)

D = 8″

The Cutline — After you have cropped a photograph, you must write a short three to five word headline (caption) about the photograph. This caption is placed above or below the picture, and sometimes is used in addition to (and above) the main cutline material. The designation "overline" is useful when you desire a line of type over the picture or over the cutline.

Cutline writing, like headline writing, is an art. You need to include more feature and descriptive information in the cutline than in the news story. Avoid giving your reader too many hard facts or belittling the reader by saying "in the above picture." Your reader knows that the cutline goes with the picture. Verbs in the cutline and caption should show action. Finally, you should consider the byline. Make it an integral part of the cutline. For example, ". . . west of the city. (Press photo by Steve Clark)."

Name_____ **Exercise 66**

PHOTO EXERCISE

Directions:

1. Use both pictures on page 233. Crop and enlarge, if necessary, each picture to fit a 3-column slot in your magazine. What will be the depth of each cut if the columns are 14-picas wide with 1 pica white space between columns?

    Top Picture: Depth_____   Bottom Picture: Depth_____

2. a. What are the depths of both pictures if they are not cropped to fit 2-column slots? The paper has 14-pica columns with 2 picas between the columns.

    Top Picture: Depth_____   Bottom Picture: Depth_____

   b. If both pictures are enlarged to fit 4-column (14-pica columns) slots, what are the enlargement percentages for both pictures?

    Top Picture: _____%   Bottom Picture: _____%

3. a. If a paper uses a 10½-pica column with ½ pica space between, what are the depths of both pictures on page 235 when those pictures are enlarged to three columns and not cropped? What are the enlargement percentages?

    Top Picture: Depth_____   Percentage_____

    Bottom Picture: Depth_____   Percentage_____

   b. Crop both pictures to fit 2-column slots. what are the depths and percentages of the cropped pictures?

    Top Picture: Depth_____   Percentage_____

    Bottom Picture: Depth_____   Percentage_____

4. Choose one of the two pictures on page 235 and make up a 50-word cutline and a four-word caption.

5. Crop the picture on page 237 to fit a 3-column slot in your newspaper. The paper has 13-pica columns with ½-pica space between. What is the depth?

    Picture: Depth_____

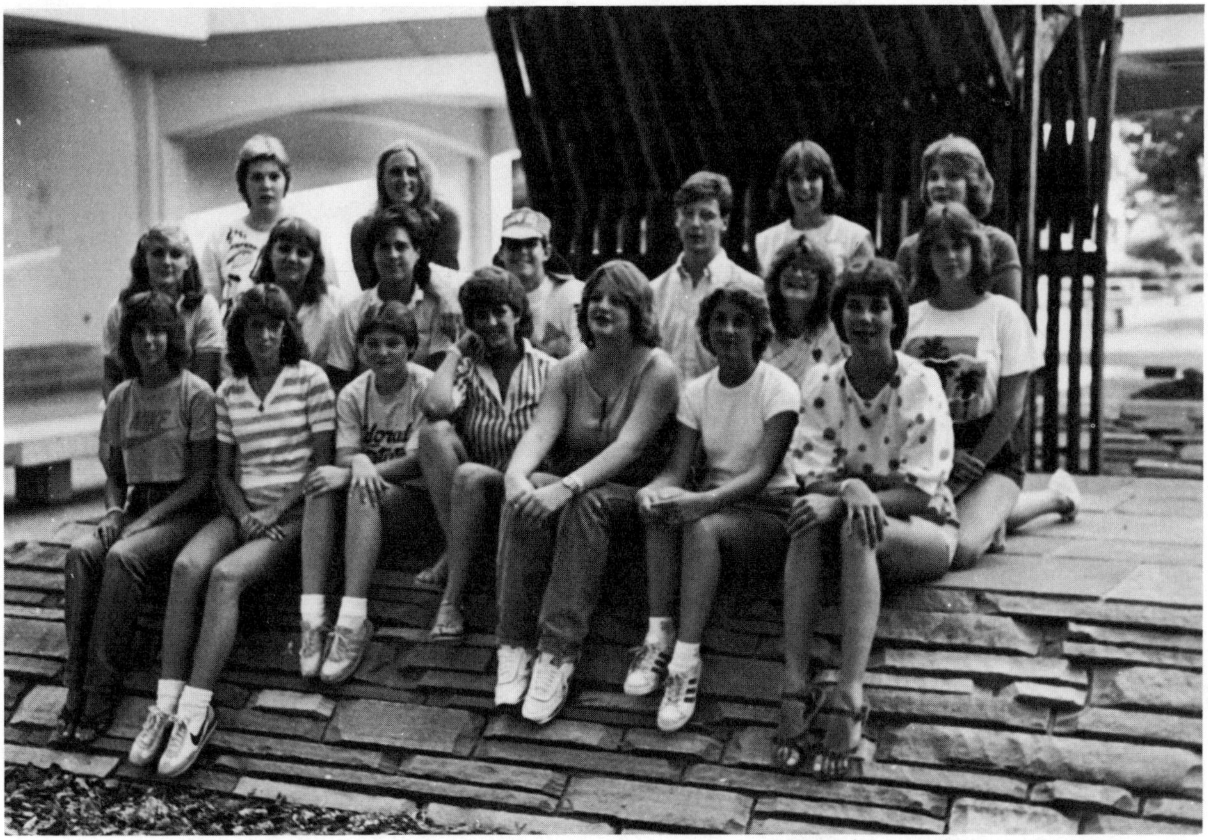

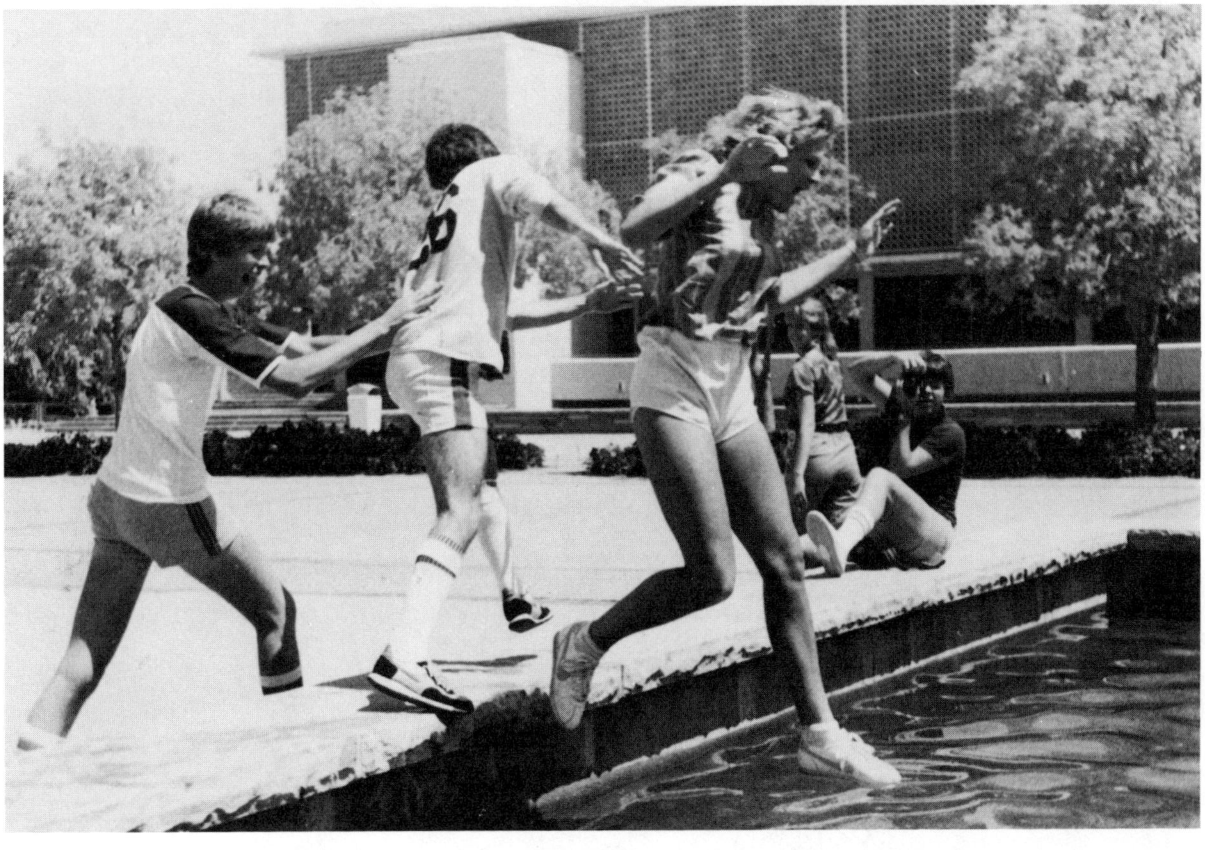

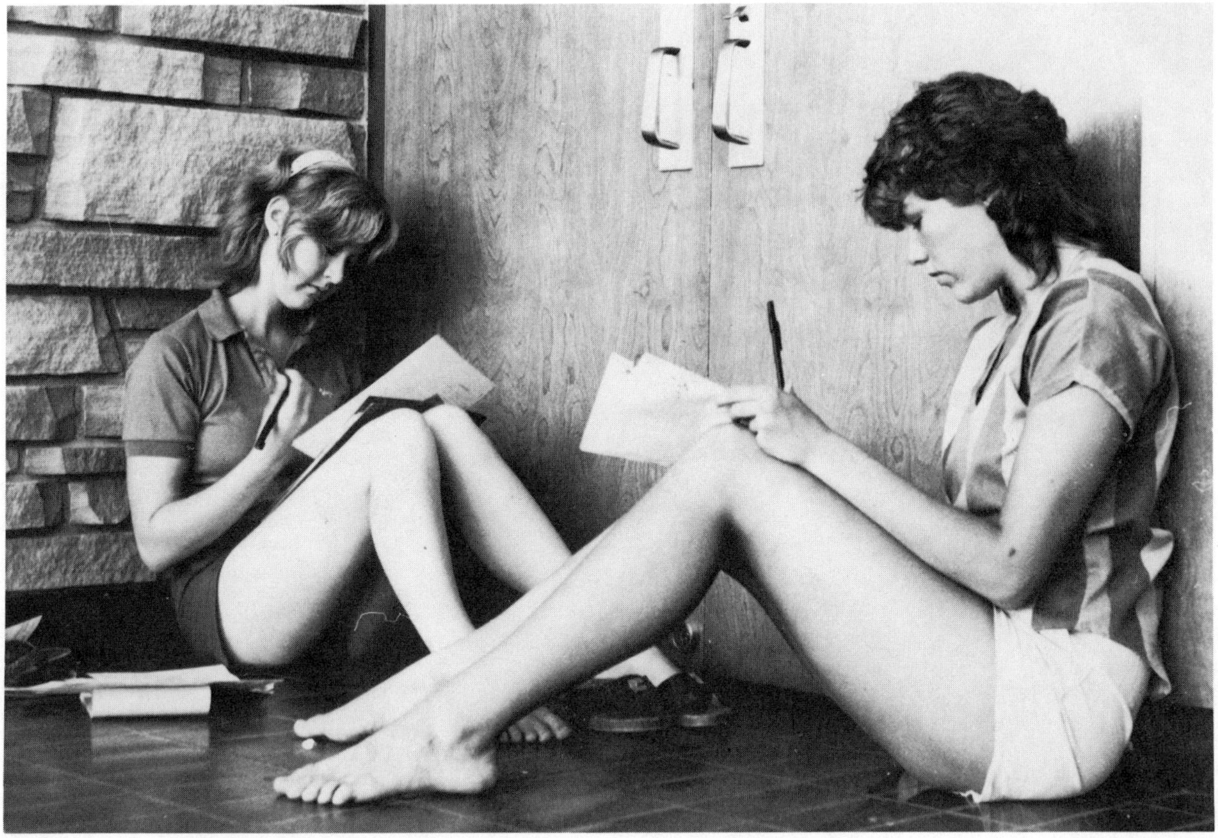

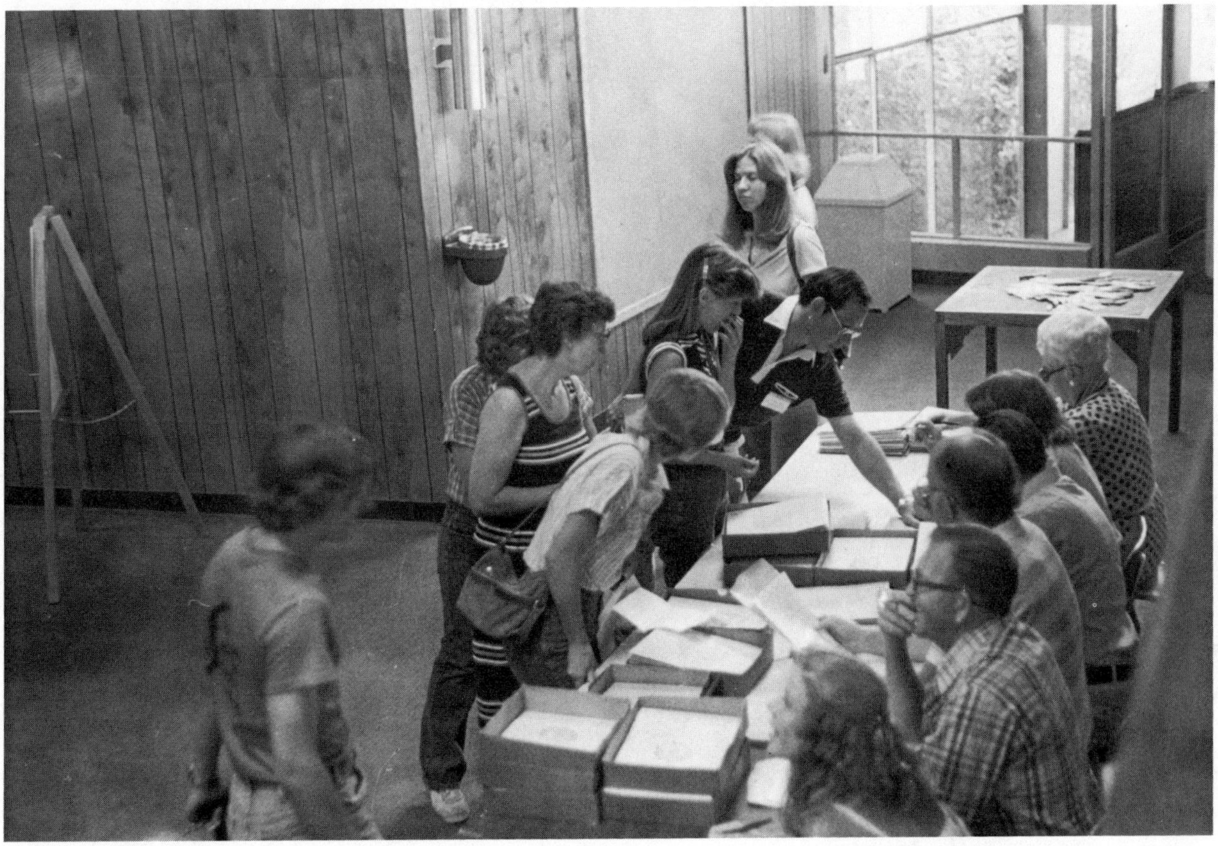

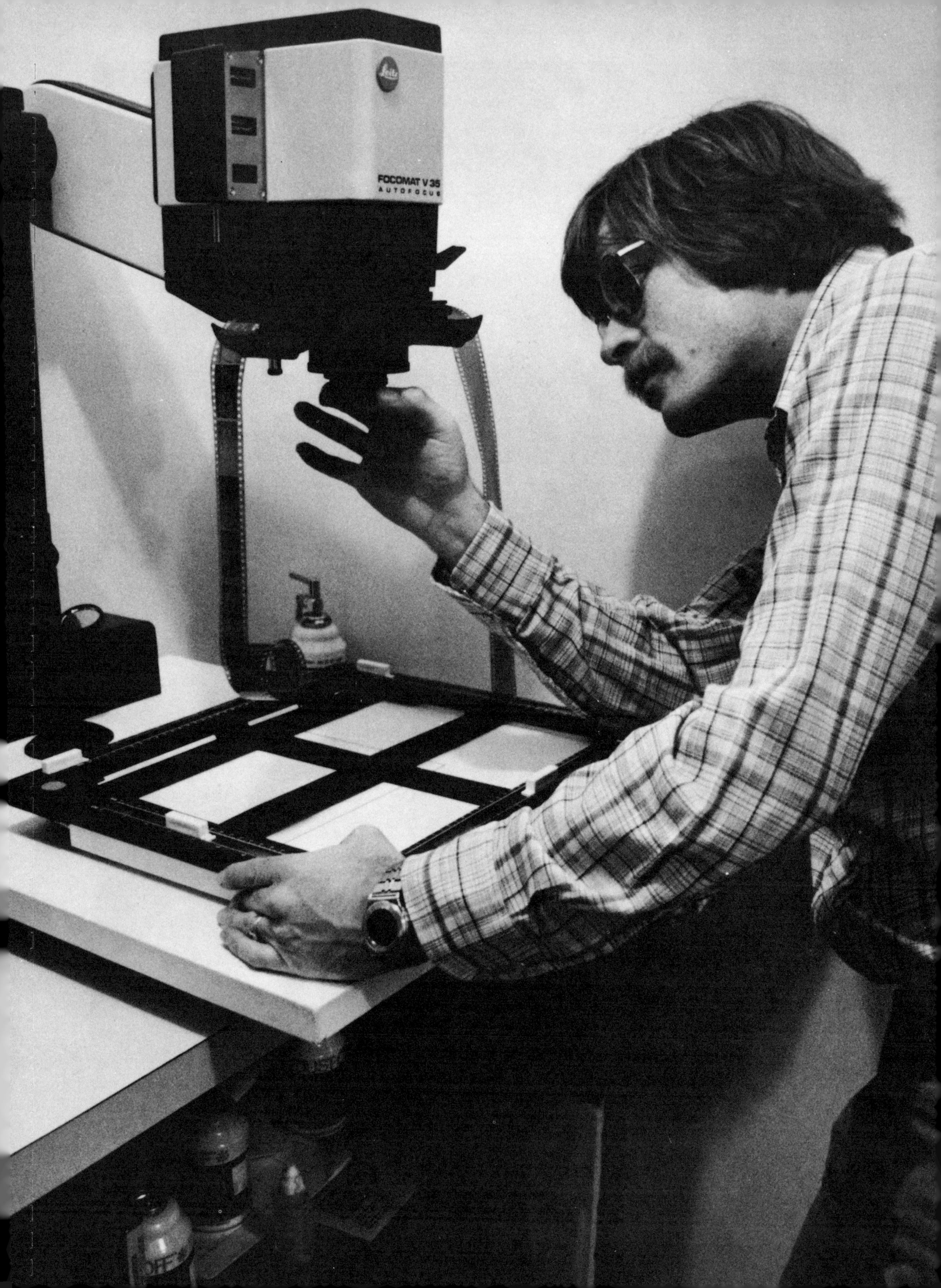
FOCOMAT V 35
AUTOFOCUS

TEMPLE DAILY TELEGRA
TEMPLE, TEXAS 76501, FRIDAY, SEPTEMBER 30, 1983
Marine Stay
Extension
Authorized
$12 Million
— To Begin Saturday —
Pilots, Flight Attendants
At Continental To Strike
— Page 2A
— McMurtry Gets No Decision —
Braves Still In Hunt
As Dodgers Fall, 7-1
— Page 1B

Chapter **13**

Makeup and Design

Makeup and design are two related but slightly different concepts as used in the newspaper industry. Makeup, as commonly conceived, is building a page element by element until all the available space is gone. Design is the completed form of that page. Ideally, the editor should have a design in mind as he or she goes through the makeup process. The makeup process includes sketching the stories, headlines, pictures and any other material that goes on a page "dummy" — a sheet of paper used to give a rough idea of placement of the various elements on the page. When the dummy is completed, it represents the page design. However, the practical distinction between design and makeup is that design indicates a greater degree of preplanning with certain elements in mind before anything is dummied on the page. Layout, then, is the actual placing of those elements on a layout page, the page used to make the printing plate.

The primary purpose of any newspaper design is to facilitate reading. In order to do this news should be packaged in contemporary, exciting and visually appealing design. Some principles that should be kept in mind in designing a page that will be visually appealing include balance, contrast, and proportion.

1) **Balance** — weighing one element with another on the opposite side of the page. To achieve an informal balance often is the ideal. Any element on the page that has visual weight must be balanced. Visual weight includes pictures, headlines, and type rules. Thus, the objective is to place heavy elements on the top and bottom and from side to side — particularly in the corners.
2) **Contrast** — using dramatically different elements. For example, to achieve contrast, you might use vertical-shaped photos with horizontal-shaped photos or light-faced headlines with ultra-bold ones. Contrast helps overcome the problem of a gray page, but overuse may cause the reader to focus on a particular element instead of the total design.
3) **Proportion** — relationships of various elements on the page. Usually unequal proportions are the most appealing. For instance, a rectangle is more pleasing to the eye than a square.

To have a total design concept that will provide page unit, you might observe several guidelines suggested by Prof. Jack Scissors of Northwestern University. They include the following:

1) Longer and fewer stories per page.
2) All stories should be square off.
3) Photos or other illustrations should be strongly vertical or horizontal.
4) Mass short stories in box or one side column.

5) Use news summaries.
6) Box at least one story on front page.
7) Look over available news and use of several designs.
8) Use 6-column format with 18 to 24 points white space between columns.

The page editor often works from a copy control sheet to design the news pages.

Other designs vary according to talent, prejudice and custom. The trend in newspaper design lately has been modular design. Modular design emphasizes horizontal makeup and working with copy and illustration blocks.

News editor must design the page using a total design concept to package the day's news. (Photo by Ft. Collins Coloradoan.)

Name_____   **Exercise 67**

Directions: The following stories are available for use on page one of a 6-column newspaper. Make up the page using as many of the stories and pictures as you need. Do not jump any story to an inside page. You may cut any story up to two inches, though. Photos may be enlarged or reduced if the same proportion is kept.

WASHINGTON — President Urges quick action on Jobs Plan. 20 inches.

NEW YORK — Severe Weather causes crisis in Northeast. 12 inches. Photo of weather scene of snow-plagued area. 4 col. x 8 inches.

CENTRAL VALLEY — School District adjusts mill levy. 10 inches.

WASHINGTON — Defense Budget cuts announced. 18 inches.

MILWAUKEE, Wis. — State Fair Sets New Attendance Record. 6 inches. Fair photo available. 3 col. x 5 inches.

MADISON — Governor urges weather modification expenditures. 8 inches.

WASHINGTON — Senate confirms attorney general nomination. 4 inches.

MADRID — 60,000 Spanish workers continue work stoppage to protest government labor policy. 10 inches with 3 col. x 6 inch photo.

PARIS — France buys 12 million tons of oil over next three years from Saudia Arabia. 6 inches.

CENTRAL VALLEY — City Planning Commission Praised by Mayor. 12 inches.

CENTRAL VALLEY — Central Valley University Seeks $50 million budget for next year — a 6.5% increase over last year. 12 inches.

Name_____ **Exercise 68**

Directions: You are news editor today on the Central Valley Free Press, an evening paper in competition with the Central Valley Tribune. The Free Press covers Collins County with emphasis on Central Valley and the immediate surrounding communities. It has a circulation of 15,000. It is now time to lay out the front page for the first edition. You have two hours until deadline. Consider the value of the stories in terms of reader-interest, significance and current news values. Plan your page so that you will bring the news into sharp focus for the tired husband, work-weary woman and busy teenager who may be reading your paper tonight.

The following are possible page one stories. The Free Press uses six 14-pica column with 2 picas of white space. It also uses 9-point type and has figured that 50 words of copy will equal about one inch when set in type. Do not jump any story. You can cut two stories, however. All pictures may be enlarged or reduced if the same proportion is kept.

CENTRAL VALLEY — Statement by the mayor on the city's refusal to participate in county COG plan. 1200 words, news.

WASHINGTON — Supreme Court rules that post office officials cannot block or detain mail to dealers in obscene material. New, 400 words.

SINGAPORE — British Prime Minister told today of his plans to sell arms to South Africa to keep from limiting any Commonwealth nation. 800 words, new.

TALLAHASSEE — Senate approves Appropriations bill 30-0. Goes to House for final approval, probably within 10 days. 750 days, mostly rewrite.

ATHENS, GA. — Two penniless sisters were found here today in their southside home where they apparently starved to death. Fragmentary details at 10 a.m. today. 200 words, new.

CENTRAL VALLEY — A university sophomore was found dead today after climbing in the mountains 15 miles west of here. Mostly rewrite from morning paper, 450 words.

WASHINGTON — The President announces the appointment of a new Secretary of Treasury. 1 col. x 3" mug shot available. 500 words, new.

ATHENS — A Greek Airlines DC-3 crashed 30 miles west of Athens killing 15 yesterday including one American. 500 words, rewrite, 2 col. x 6" photo accompanies wire story.

LOS ANGELES — A 2 col. x 8" pix of Chinese lifting winning U.S. gymnastic team member to shoulders after she beat the Chinese. 150 word cutline.

WASHINGTON — Tax bill approved by House. Would reduce taxes for middle-income if passed by Senate and signed by President. New, 1000 words.

Name _____   **Exercise 69**

Directions: Make up a front page using some or all of the following stories. Do not jump any story and do not cut more than two inches from any story. The front page is 5 columns of 12 picas each with 1 pica space between columns.

1. Snow claims one life in freak spring storm in Montana; 8 inches.
2. Bullets, rockets Threaten Mideast Peace; 13 inches.
3. Texas Governor to testify before Judiciary committee; 12 inches.
4. President to address nation on summer energy problems; 8 inches.
5. Democrats win in special New Jersey election; 6 inches.
6. School official in Central Valley resigns under pressure; 12 inches.
7. Syrians welcome U.S. Secretary of State; 8 inches.
8. Tax Bill signed by governor; 16 inches.
9. County appoints interim finance director; 6 inches.
10. Local city council elects mayor; 10 inches.

Pictures:

2 col. by 8 inch cut of Central Valley University student testifying before Senate committee on dirty tricks. (You may change size if you keep the same proportion.)

2 col. by 5 inch cut of council electing new mayor. (You may change the width and depth if you keep same proportion.)

3 col. by 6 inch cut of circus in town yesterday. (Change if needed.)

Name _____ **Exercise 70**

Directions: Use the following stories for one of your wire pages. (6-col. page) Edit the attached story, write the headline you assign, and make up the page. You may cut any of the following stories by as much as 2 inches; use only those stories you consider most newsworthy.

DENVER — Colorado Supreme Court rules on conflict of interest suit against Denver district attorney. 10 inches.

WASHINGTON — President signs compromise energy bill. 18 inches

WASHINGTON — Democratic congressmen meet to draw up bill to end oil depletion allowance. 8 inches

LOS ANGELES — Catholic schools show decline; rate of decline decreases, however. 12 inches

WASHINGTON — ERDA may excavate contaminated mud in Ohio. 14 inches

ATLANTA — Wirephoto of rescue attempt across flooded river. Photo is 3 columns by 6 inches. You may reduce or enlarge, but keep the same proportions.

NEW YORK — John F. Kennedy, Jr. robbed of bicycle. 8 inches

WASHINGTON — Sen. John Tower, R-Texas, lists $428,000 in campaign gifts for this year's election. 1 col. by 3 inch mug shot with 8-inch story.

YELLOWSTONE, Wyo. — Yellowstone Park opened for visitors today. 4 inches

MEMPHIS — Photo of light plane crash that killed one person. 3 col. x 5 inches with 6 inches of copy that can be used as story or cutline. Photo may be enlarged or reduced if same proportion kept.

DALLAS — President speaks at dedication of new convention center. Calls for massive effort by big business to create new jobs. 10 inches

CHICAGO — $4.5 million in cocaine found in car of two teenagers from New York who were stopped by police for speeding on the freeway near downtown. 5 inches

Name_____ **Exercise 71**

Directions: Assume you are the city editor for the Central Valley *Free Press.* You have the following stories to use to design the first page of the city section. The *Free Press* uses 6-column makeup (14 pica columns with 2 pica space between) for the first page of any section of the paper. You may cut any story up to 5 inches, and you may reduce or enlarge the photos if the same proportion is kept.

*City Humane Society recommends new city ordinance to City Council to regulate cats. 10 inches.

*County Commissioners sign new computer agreement with city. 8 inches.

*City Council to discuss new library site at tomorrow's meeting — advance story also highlighting other major agenda items. 18 inches.

*Feature story on new city planner. 1 col. x 3 inch mug shot. 15 inches.

*2 col. x 8 inch photo of new plaque being attached to first church building in Central Valley. (One-inch cutline with photo telling story)

*News feature on use of dogs by city policemen. 17 inches with a 3 col. x 6 inch cut of dog with policeman on beat.

*Human interest story about visitors to fire station. 6 inches.

*State Senator Van Hart to speak at Central Valley University commencement exercises next week. 8 inches.

Name_____ **Exercise 72**

Directions: Use the following copy to dummy the front page of the Central Valley *Free Press* sports page. You may cut any story up to 4 inches, and you may reduce or enlarge the photos proportionally. First page of the sports section is 6 columns, 14 picas wide with 2 picas of white space between columns.

1. Bob Unser wins Indianapolis 500. 20 inches with 5 col. x 4½ inch cut of winner and car in winner's circle.

2. Boston Celtics win NBA championship by defeating Los Angeles Lakers in four straight games. 18 inches with 2 col. x 8 inch cut of Celtic players after the game.

3. Sidebar story. Jo Jo White named most valuable player of NBA championship series. 3 col. x 10 inch cut of White driving to the basket during final game. 8 inch story.

4. Sports column. 20 inches.

5. Track meet between City High and Grover High. City High wins. 10 inches.

6. City volleyball championship series begins tonight. 8 inches.

7. CVU signs top high school running back to letter of intent for next year. 7 inches with 1 col. x 3 inch mug shot.

Name_____ **Exercise 73**

Directions: Use the following stories and photos to dummy the second sports page for today's Central Valley *Free Press*. You may cut any story by as much as 4 inches; photos may be enlarged or reduced in proportion. You may use any stories you had left over from the front page of the sports section. Inside pages are 8 cols. 10½ picas with ½ pica space between columns.

1. CVU tops CU in wrestling. 8 inches.

2. Fishing feature. 22 inches. 2 col. x 6 inch photo of fly fisherman.

3. Local softball results. 8 inches.

4. Baseball results (wire roundup of pro baseball). 12 inches.

5. Track story on local prospects for this year's conference championship meet coming up next week. Picture of pole vaulter who won district last year; he placed third in the state meet last year. 14 inches with a 2 col. x 8 inch photo.

6. Wirephoto and story of in third loss of the season without any victories. Story is 8 inches. Photo is 2 col. x 5 inches.

7. Spring football practice continues at CVU. 10-inch report with 3 col. x 6 inch photo.

COPY CONTROL SHEET

Editor _____   Edition _____

Story Slug	Page	Inches of story	Headline size	Copy Editor

Editor:_____   Page:_____

Editor:_____   Page:_____

Editor:_____   Page:_____

Editor: _____   Page: _____

Editor: _____   Page: _____

Editor:_____   Page:_____

Editor: _____   Page: _____

Editor:_____   Page:_____

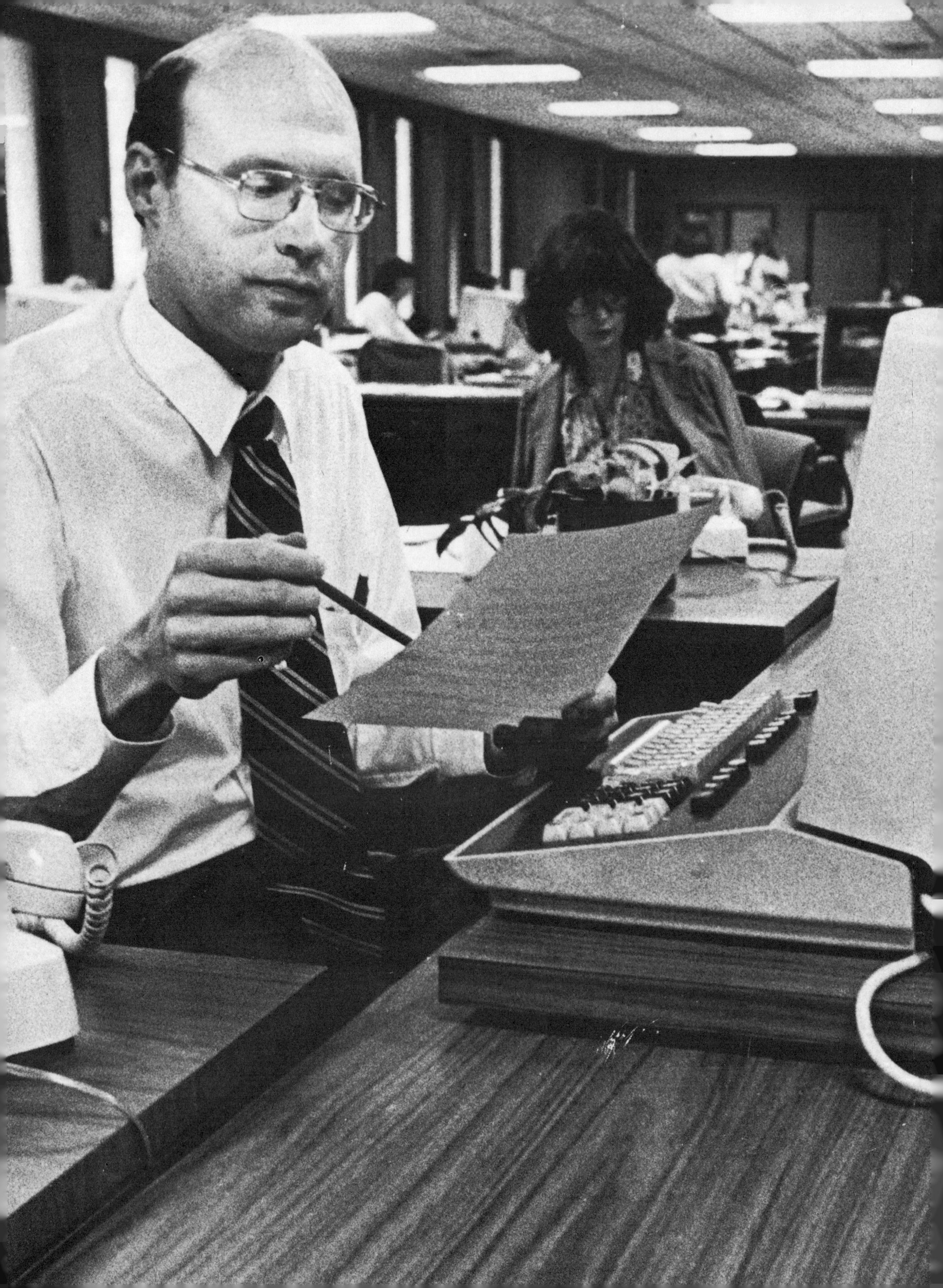

Chapter 14

Proofreading

In most cases the copy editor and the proofreader are two distinct jobs. Sometimes, though, the copy editor may have to read proof. Such cases include times when copy has been overset or when certain stories require last-minute updating. Most proofreading in today's newspaper offices is done on the visual display terminal. However, just like editing there are times when you may need to do proofreading with a pencil. Public relations practitioners often use proofreading marks in proofing brochures, pamphlets, internal publications and other print media.

After copy has been edited and set in type, a "proof" of the copy is pulled. A proofreader then reads the proof copy and checks it against the edited version to make sure that it conforms to the edited copy.

Another responsibility for the proofreader (and makeup editor) is to check page proofs. Usually the reader checks only major elements such as the following:

1. Have major proofreading corrections been made from the galley proofs?
2. Are headlines over the right stories?
3. Are dates/issue numbers correct?
4. Are sluglines removed?
5. Are pictures right side up?

Newspapers use an informal proofreading method in contrast to formal methods of book publishers. Newspapers make all corrections in the nearest margin with a line drawn to the error in the typeset copy. The following are some of the major proofreading marks used:

lc	lower case	≡	capitalize letter
ital	set in italics	tr	transpose letters/words
lf	light face	bf	set in boldface
⌒	close up	#	space
¶	new paragraph	no ¶	no paragraph
a/	add a letter	⌿	delete a letter
∧	insert period	∧	insert comma
v	insert apostrophe	:	insert colon
v"	insert quote marks	=/	insert hyphen
sp	spell out	eq#	equalize space between words

273

Name_____ **Exercise 74**

Proofreading Exercise

Directions: Use the following as edited copy to read proof on the typeset story. Make the proper proofreading corrections on the typeset copy.

[An estimated $6,500.~~00~~ was caused friday in a fire at 4024 Crown Dr.] (damage above)

[Firemen sa*id* they responded to a~~laarm~~ *alarm* at the home of T*h*omas Hellman at 12:27 P.M.] (R.)

Reports said the fire was igni*t*ed on a mattress in a (2nd) floor bedroom, possibly by children playing with matches.

Units from the Central Valley Fire department responded to the call. No injuries were reported.

    An estimated $6,500.oo damge was caused Friday at 4021 Crown Drive.
    Firemen said they responded to an alarm at the home of Thomas Hellman at 12:27 P.m.
    Report said the fire was ignited on a amttress in a second-floor bedroom possibly by children playing with matches.
    Units from the Central Valley Fire department responded to the call. No injuries were reported.

Name_____ **Exercise 75**

Proofreading Exercise

Directions: From the following edited story proofread the typeset copy and make it conform to the edited story.

College Avenue from Oak Street to Johnson Avenue may be closed to through-traffic within the next year if a consultant's plan on downtown revitalization is adopted by the city council.

That proposal is among the major downtown revisions recommended in a report compiled by Research Associates of Dallas.

The report calls for numerous renovations in the six-block central business district including rerouting through-traffic from College to Remington street.

Remington now stops at a deadend juncture with Pine Avenue, and its extension would entail plowing through the small triangular block on the north side of Pine.

Renewed interest in downtown renovation is prompted by growth of Central Valley as an economic center for the region.

"It is clear that within the next fifteen years, Central Valley will be able to support one or two additional 'shopping centers' on the scale of the Westcliff Mall, and there is no reason why one of these could not be a revitalized and expanded downtown retail function," the report states.

"The Central Valley area will continue to grow, most likely at a rate greater than the general economy of the large northern Colorado region if Central Valley chooses to capitalize on its potential as a regional center," the consultants added.

The report released today by Norm Feit, city consultant, also calls for special treatment on Trinidad and Peterson streets and for open space and pedestrian emphasis in the downtown area.

Trinidad is recommended for treatment as a "special identity" street with "generous landscaping" to connect the downtown with Central Valley University.

Sidewalk landscaping, five-foot bikelanes separated by a 1-1/2-foot raised median, parking and two lanes of traffic are recommended for Peterson improvements.

277

The street improvements, the rerouting of College traffic and pedestrianways and plazas, are cited by the consultants as the mechanisms for setting the stage for downtown redevelopment.

The recommended actions and priorities portion of the 150-page report recommends an immediate phase of implementation, which includes:

*Design and construction of a parking mall on College, a Peterson Street pedestrian linkage between Trinidad and Library Park, and designation of a "central place" or focal point on the southwest side of the intersection of College and Peterson.

*Initiating development of a railroad yard area between Trinidad and the retail core area, in office and supporting services.

*Making provisions for 300 additional off-street parking spaces by next year and another 300 by the end of the year.

*Completion of the auditorium and City Hall facilities as the pace of planning permits.

*Development of additional downtown office facilities, resolution of the library site issue and construction of the new $1.6 million library.

-30-

College Avenue from Oak Street to Johnson Avenue may be closed to through-traffic within the next year if a consultant's plan on downtown revitalization is adopted by the city council.

That proposal is among the major downtown revisions recommended in a report compiled by Research Associates of Dallas.

The report calls for numerous renovations in the six-clock central business district including rerouting through-traffic from College to Remington Street.

Remington now stops at a deadend juncture with Pine Avenue and its extension would entail plowing through the small triangular block on the north side of Pine.

Renewed interest in downtown renovation is prompted by growth of Central Valley as an economic center for the region.

"It is clear that within the next fifteen years, Central Valley will be able to support one or two additional 'shoping centers' on the scale of the Westcliff Mall, and there is no reason why one of these could not be a revitalized and expanded downtown retail function," the report states. "The Central Valley area will continue to grow, most likely at a rate greater than the general economy of the larger northern Colorado region if Central Valley chooses to capitalize on its potential as a regional center," the consultants added.

The report released today by Norm Feit, city consultant, also calls for special treatment on Triniday and Peterson Streets and for open space and pedestrian emphasis in the downtown area.

Trinidad is recommended for treatment as a "special identity" street with "generous landscaping" to connect the downtown with Central Valley University.

Sidewald landscaping, five-foot bikelands separated by a 1½-foot raised median, parking and two lanes of traffic are recommended for Peterson improvements. The street improvements, the rerouting of College traffic and pedestrianways and plazas, are cited by the consultants as the mechanisms for setting the stage for downtown redevelopment.

The recommended actions and priorities portion of the 150-page report recommends an immediate phase of implementation, which includes:

*Design and construction of a parking mall on college, an Peterson Street pedestrial linkage between Trinidad and Library Park, and designation of a "central place" or focal point on the southwest side of the intersection of College and Peterson.

*Initiating development of a railroad yard area between Trinidad and the retail core area, in office and supporting services.

*Making provisions for 300 addition off-street parking spaces by next year and another 300 by the end of 1990.

*Completion of the auditorium and City Hall facilities as the pace of planning permits.

*Development of additional downtown office facilities, resolution of the library site issue and construction of the new $1.6 million library.

-30-

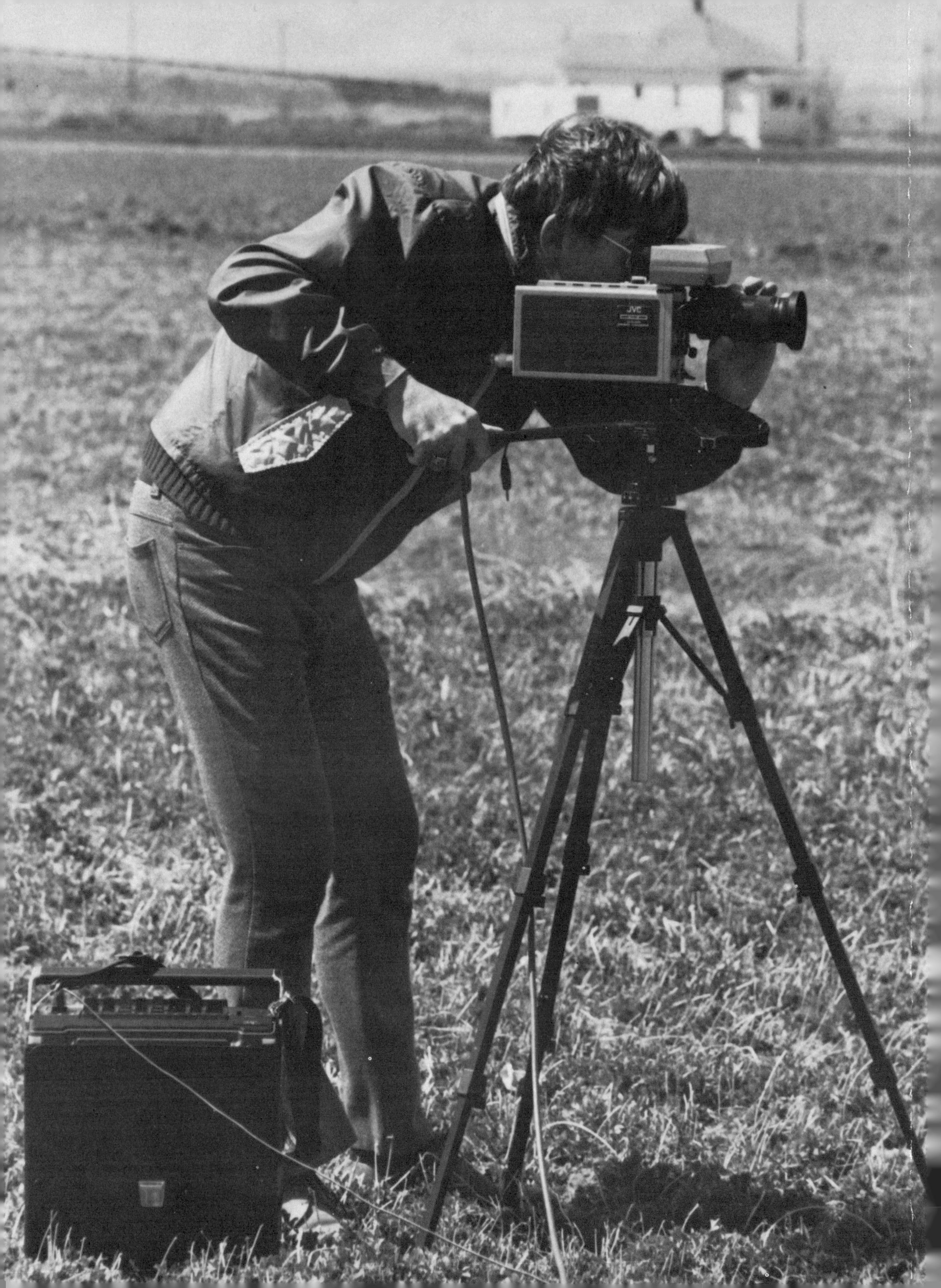
JVC

Chapter 15

Broadcast News Editing

Editing is just as important for the electronic news media as it is for print. While similar mistakes must be avoided in all media, several editing differences exist.

Primarily, the news must be edited for the ear in electronic media; therefore, the writing style must be sound-oriented. Rhythm is important. For instance, leads must be quite short, and repetition of specific items may be needed in certain stories. Second, the newscaster must be particularly careful to produce clean copy either through retyping or clearly making the copy changes. In most cases edited material should be retyped. Most newspaper editing marks should not be used in broadcast editing. Copy editing symbols are used as shorthand between the copy editor and the production department in the print media. A broadcast journalist, on the other hand, does not have time to translate the symbols when reading copy on the air. For similar reasons, broadcast style is different from newspaper style. For example, most abbreviations should be eliminated, capitalization should be used freely, and words requiring emphasis should be underlined (see the broadcast style guidelines at the end of this chapter).

The following editing changes may be made in broadcast copy; other editing will require retyping the story:

1) Material may be eliminated by completely blacking it out.

    Example: Officials said school ~~school~~ would open today.

2) Entire words may be changed by blacking out the word(s) and inserting the new word. Individual letters cannot be inserted.

    Example: Officials ~~sied~~ *said* school would open today.

3) Limited new material may be added.

    Example: Officials *said school* would open today.

The radio and television newscast format should build interest in the audience by consistent good quality. Placement of stories (format) should be determined carefully to create the desired effect. Unlike the newspaper which places its major news on page one, the broadcast format must be arranged to sustain interest throughout the show. However, the lead story almost always is the one judged most significant of the day even though the broadcast lead story may not agree with the newspaper banner story for the day. Unlike the banner head of a newspaper, which is used to attract an audience, the broadcast news audience is already tuned in and the lead story will not add to the audience. On a television broadcast it is usually best to lead with a story that has a visual (videotape, film or slides). The news format should be calculated to have good pace, style and personality.

To achieve good pace, the news broadcaster should lead with a significant story. Next, however, the broadcaster should remember that the audience cannot remain at an overexcitement pitch throughout the broadcast; therefore, the broadcaster should give the audience time to relax (a change of pace) before presenting another top story that may be particularly stimulating. The ending is a key element of the news broadcast. The broadcaster should try not to end on an unpleasant note, but instead should conclude with a brief feature if possible. On television it's desirable to end with a good visual story. The basic structure of a news broadcast, then, is "wave action" with peaks and valleys of interest. The climax is at or near the beginning, but there are many lesser climaxes. This does not mean that "hard" news necessarily is held until later in the show. Normally, hard news elements diminish as the show progresses and feature content increases. Another way to give a change of pace beside different content is to change talent. In a radio broadcast this may be switching to a taped report (actuality) from a reporter at the city council or the governor's office. For a television broadcast, a switch from the anchorman to a film reporter on location provides a good change of pace. Another way to change pace is to vary the format. For example, after a long story follow with a series of short items.

To put a radio news broadcast together, the broadcaster must read all available news copy, select and edit the most important stories for use on the broadcast, and time the material to fit the available news time. Using a 65-space line, 16 lines of copy will take about one minute of air time to present. Most broadcasters "backtime" the last two or three items, note the time on the copy, and include some "pad copy" in case time is left after the last item.

Television broadcasts are prepared similar to a radio broadcast, but because of the visuals, more is involved in television. The format is determined best by deciding first where to put major visuals, filling in with copy to be read on camera, and finally placing commercials where they interfere least with the continuity of the program. The commercial is the one built-in transition; it can serve as a natural break for a change from news to weather, for example. There are several possible lead-ins to a commercial. These include:

1) Direct cut from news to commercial.
2) Picture fades to black between news and commercial.
3) Title slide of station between news and commercial.
4) Newsman delivers short lead in such as "more news in a minute..." or "Coming up next..."

The later three transitions are better than the first. The first provides no transition and may cause the viewer trouble in distinguishing news from advertising. The second method gives a short pause and provides transition; however, some producers object. Providing a title slide of a couple of seconds between news and commercials is good transition, but it is harder on the director and may give more chance for error. Letting the newsman provide the lead-in may be good if well done, but it can actually cause the viewer to lose interest if he doesn't like what is coming up next.

To prepare the television news show the following steps should be undertaken:

1) Choose stories, edit, proofread, and time for length.
2) Decide the order of stories, stack, script commercial breaks and transition to sports, weather, etc.

3) Do videotape line-up sheet and block-in filmed commercials.
4) Put videotape and commercials in order.
5) Break down copy and number pages.
6) Put flips and other visuals in order and number.
7) Do format sheet listing all elements of newscast, individual times and accumulative times for the show.
8) Check copy against videotape order.
9) Check film order against videotape line-up sheet (including commercials).
10) Check flips and visuals for order.
11) Backtime finishing copy.
12) Prepare pad copy.
13) Rehearse and time show.
14) Mark copy — three scripts (director, anchor, and producer).
15) Delivery copy to director, anchor, and producer.
16) Deliver the newscast.

BROADCAST STYLE GUIDELINES

1. All copy must be typewritten on standard size paper.
2. Triple space.
3. Type on only one side of the paper.
4. Use 65-space line. (Set margins at 10 and 75.) When timing your copy, 16 lines will equal about one minute of air time.
5. Put slug in upper left corner of page.
6. Start story about four to six lines below the slug.
7. Paragraph story as frequently as needed for sense and unity.
8. Indent paragraphs five spaces.
9. Use end mark (### or -30-) at the end of the story.
10. If the story continues to second page, either write "more" and circle it at the bottom of the page or draw a long arrow pointing to the next page. Never carry part of a sentence or paragraph over to another page.
11. Put only one story on a page.
12. Omit datelines.
13. Underline words that require special emphasis or words that may be difficult to pronounce.
14. Never split words or hyphenated phrases from one line to the next. Care must be exercised in how a line of copy ends. For example,

    "Looking at the forecast, snow and cold
    weather seem to be heading our way."

    The news reader would stop after saying the word "cold" thinking that was the end of a thought, and would stumble on finding the weather "weather" at the start of the next line.
15. Eliminate most abbreviations. Exceptions, Mr., Mrs., Dr.; commonly abbreviated groups such as Y-M-C-A or U-N; and time designations.
16. Capitalize freely.
17. Spell out figures under 10; use numerals 10 through 999; use hyphenated combinations for numerals and words above 999 (e.g., 33-thousand).
18. Round off numbers unless exact number is significant.
19. Use st, rd, th, and nd after dates, addresses, and those numbers to be read as ordinary numbers; 2nd, 116th street.
20. In age references, say 21-year-old.
21. Follow traditional punctuation; however, question marks should be used only when needed for inflection.
22. Use direct quotes sparingly. Never use the words quote, unquote, and quotation. Set off quote with such phrases as in these words, in her words, as he put it, her exact words were.
23. Use phoenetic spelling for words of difficult pronunciation.
24. Do not begin a story with a name.
25. Titles precede the name. It's always, "Secretary of State Schultz says the U.S. must meet its world commitments." Never, "The U.S. must meet its world commitments, Secretary Schultz says."
26. Use complete name in the first reference except the Pope or the president.
27. Omit obscure names and places if not meaningful to the story.
28. Strive for use of present tense, but don't force it. It is better to use past tense if needed.
29. Avoid repetition of time element today.
30. Use transition sparingly. Instead, many writers use a lot of dots . . . . . to give the copy air . . . . and also provide visual cues for a TV newscaster who must glance up from his or her copy, and then find the place again when looking back.

Name_____ **Exercise 76**

Directions: Edit for a radio broadcast.

FLIER MISSING

RADIO WIRE

A WHYOMING FLIER MISSING SINCE MONDAY STUMBLED INTO A RANCH THREE MILES SOUTH OF WOODS LANDING IN NORTHERN COLORADO TODAY.

THIRTY-SIX-YEAR-OLD BRUCE DAVIS, WHOSE PLANE CRASHED IN THE SNOW THREE DAYS AGO, SAID, "I'M ALL RIGHT."

HE LEFT HIS WIFE, UNABLE TO WALK, AT THE PLANE. A RESCUE PARTY STARTED FOR HER AT ONCE. DAVIS ADDED, "I DON'T KNOW HOW SHE IS."

HE SET OUT WITH STATE POLICE TO RETURN TO THE PLANE. IT APPARENTLY WAS SOME DISTANCE SOUTH OF LARAMIE, WYOMING NEAR BULL MOUNTAIN.

DAVIS WAS FLYING FROM SALT LAKE CITY TO DENVER WHEN HE SENT A RADIO APPEAL TO THE C-A-T AT STAPLETON AT 3:30 P-M MONDAY, SAYING HE WAS LOST IN THE CLOUDS AND NEEDED RADIO HELP TO GET IN. THAT WAS THE LAST HEARD FROM HIM UNTIL THIS MORNING.

DAVIS SAID "WE HIT ABOUT 4 O'CLOCK. I PUT THE PLANE BETWEEN TWO TREES AND THEY TORE THE WINGS OFF BUT ACTED AS A BUMPER."

HE SAID HIS WIFE RECEIVED A BLOW ON THE HEAD BUT DID NOT LOSE CONSCIOUSNESS.

DAVIS WENT ON TO SAY:

"I MOVED HER LEGS AND DETERMINED THEY WERE NOT BROKEN, BUT SHE COULD NOT WALK. I SAID I HAD BETTER START RIGHT OUT.

"I WRAPPED HER UP IN EVERYTHING I COULD FIND, THEN LEFT."

THAT WAS THREE DAYS AGO. HE HAD WANDERED THROUGH THE MILE-HIGH MOUNTAINS OF THE AREA, 30 MILES SOUTHWEST OF LARAMIE, SINCE THEN, LOOKING FOR A ROAD OR RANCH.

"I'M WORN OUT," HE SAID, "BUT BASICALLY I'M ALL RIGHT. TOO MUCH WALKING."

THE GUS ROBERTSON RANCH AT WHICH DAVIS ARRIVED AT 6:10 A.M. TODAY IS THREE MILES SOUTH OF WOODS LANDING AND ABOUT 35 MILES EAST OF THE POINT WHERE AERIAL SEARCH FOR HIS PLANE HAD CENTERED YESTERDAY.

###

Name _____ **Exercise 77**

Directions: Edit the following story for a radio broadcast.

PYTHON

FORT WORTH, Texas, Sept. 13 — an eighteen foot python named Pete was free and on the prowl Saturday and a police sound truck drove around the zoo blaring "There's a dangerous snake on the loose."

Harry Jackson, the snake's caretaker, said Pete really isn't dangerous at all — unless of course somebody steps on him. Zoo employees and policemen clared Forest Park and began a thoro search for the big snake, which kills it's food by coiling around it and crushing it.

Pete was brought to the zoo four years ago from Bangkok, Thailand. The reptile is nearly a foot in diameter and weighs several hundred pounds. Pete's absence from his ca ge was dis covered at 9:30A.M. today. About 4,000 persons were in the zoo grounds when Pete's disappearence was discovered by his caretaker.

222pafg. . .

Directions: Edit the following story for a radio broadcast.

PILGRIMAGE

After a week of local activities that including singing, square dancing and quilting exhibitions, the Collins County entry in teh Wagon Train Pilgrimage got under way this weekend.

The wagon, its drivers and outriders were given a sendoff early Saturday in flag-rainsing ceremonies at the Elks Club, 140 East Oak Street. The wagon train then paraded down College Avenue and onto Warren Park where lunch was served. The group spent the neight at the County Fairgrounds in and is expected to reach the Essex County fairgrounds early this afternoon.

From there it will travel to Raton Pass where the wagon is scheduled to join wagons from other western states near the end of the month. They, in turn, plan to join wagons from all 50 states at Valley Forge, for ceramonies on July 4.

-30-

Name_____ **Exercise 78**

Directions: Select and edit copy for a 5-minute noon radio newscast from last night's newspaper. Use the format sheet to schedule the stories, commercials, and pad copy. Write out your transition copy.

News Format

	T	A

T = time of individual item.
A = running total.

Appendix A

Copy Editing Symbols

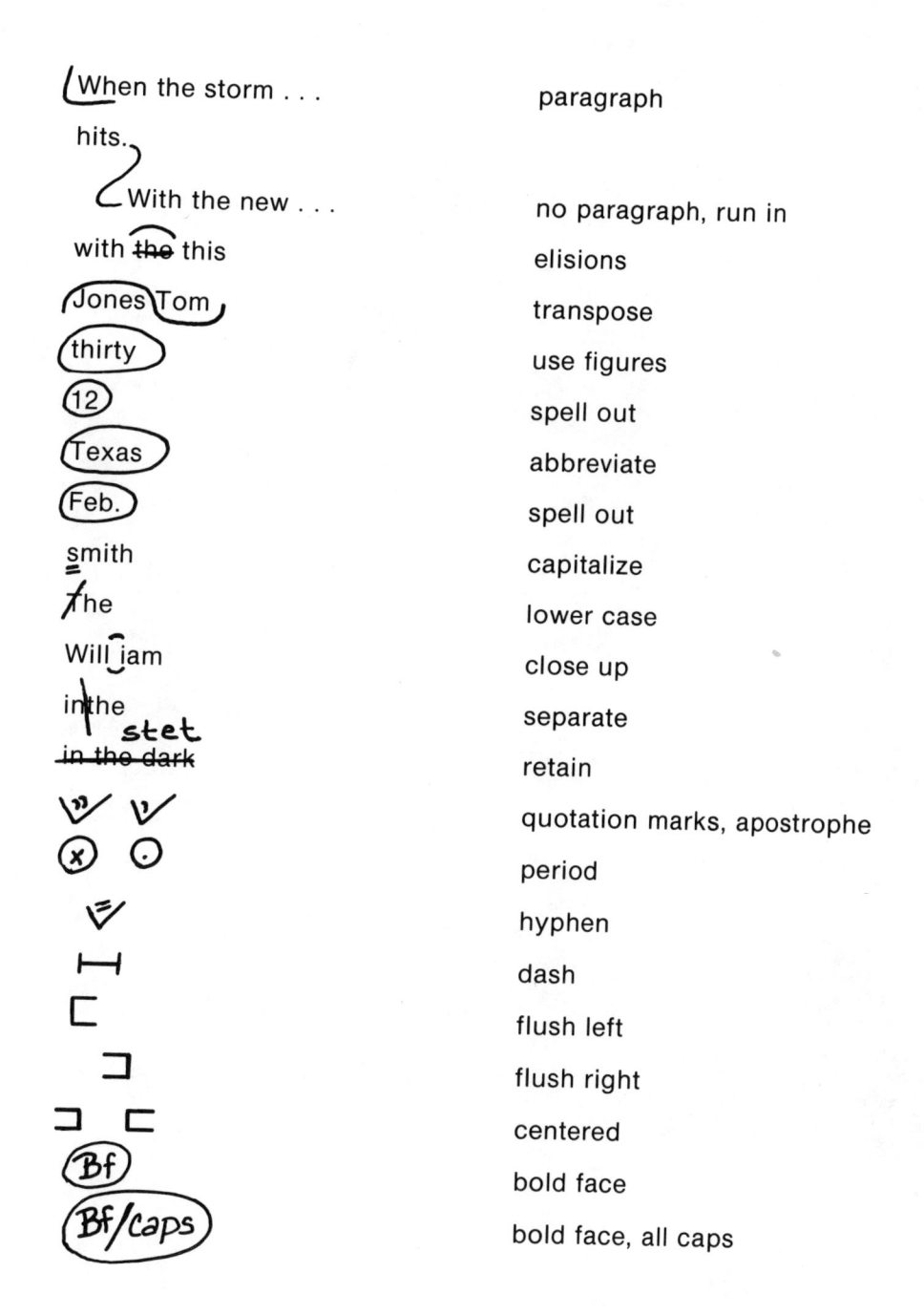

⌐When the storm . . . hits. ⌐With the new . . .	paragraph
	no paragraph, run in
with ~~the~~ this	elisions
Jones Tom	transpose
(thirty)	use figures
(12)	spell out
(Texas)	abbreviate
(Feb.)	spell out
smith	capitalize
/The	lower case
Will⌣iam	close up
in|the	separate
~~in the dark~~ stet	retain
ⱽ ⱽ	quotation marks, apostrophe
⊗ ⊙	period
ⱽ	hyphen
⊢⊣	dash
⌐	flush left
⌐	flush right
⌐ ⌐	centered
(Bf)	bold face
(Bf/caps)	bold face, all caps

Appendix B
Headline Schedule

(Count expressed is maximum possible for head size and column width; minimum acceptable usually is two counts below maximum.)

I. 8-COLUMN FORMAT (11 pica columns)

Point	1 col	2 col	3 col	4 col	5 col	6 col	7 col	8 col
14	20	39	—	—	—	—	—	—
18	14	28	42	—	—	—	—	—
24	11	24	36	49	—	—	—	—
30	9	18	28	37	47	—	—	—
36	—	16	24	33	42	50	59	67
48	—	—	17	22	28	33	39	45
60	—	—	—	18	22	27	31	36
72	—	—	—	—	20	24	27	31

II. 6-COLUMN FORMAT (14 pica columns)

Point	1 col	2 col	3 col	4 col	5 col	6 col
14	27	55	83	—	—	—
18	23	47	71	95	—	—
24	16	33	50	67	84	—
30	12	25	38	51	64	77
36	—	21	32	43	54	65
48	—	16	24	32	40	48
60	—	—	—	26	32	39
72	—	—	—	—	—	32

III. 5-COLUMN FORMAT (12 pica columns)

Point	1 col	2 col	3 col	4 col	5 col
14	22	45	—	—	—
18	16	33	50	—	—
24	13	27	40	44	—
30	10	21	32	42	53
36	9	19	29	38	47
48	—	—	18	25	32
60	—	—	—	20	24
72	—	—	—	—	22

Appendix C

State Map

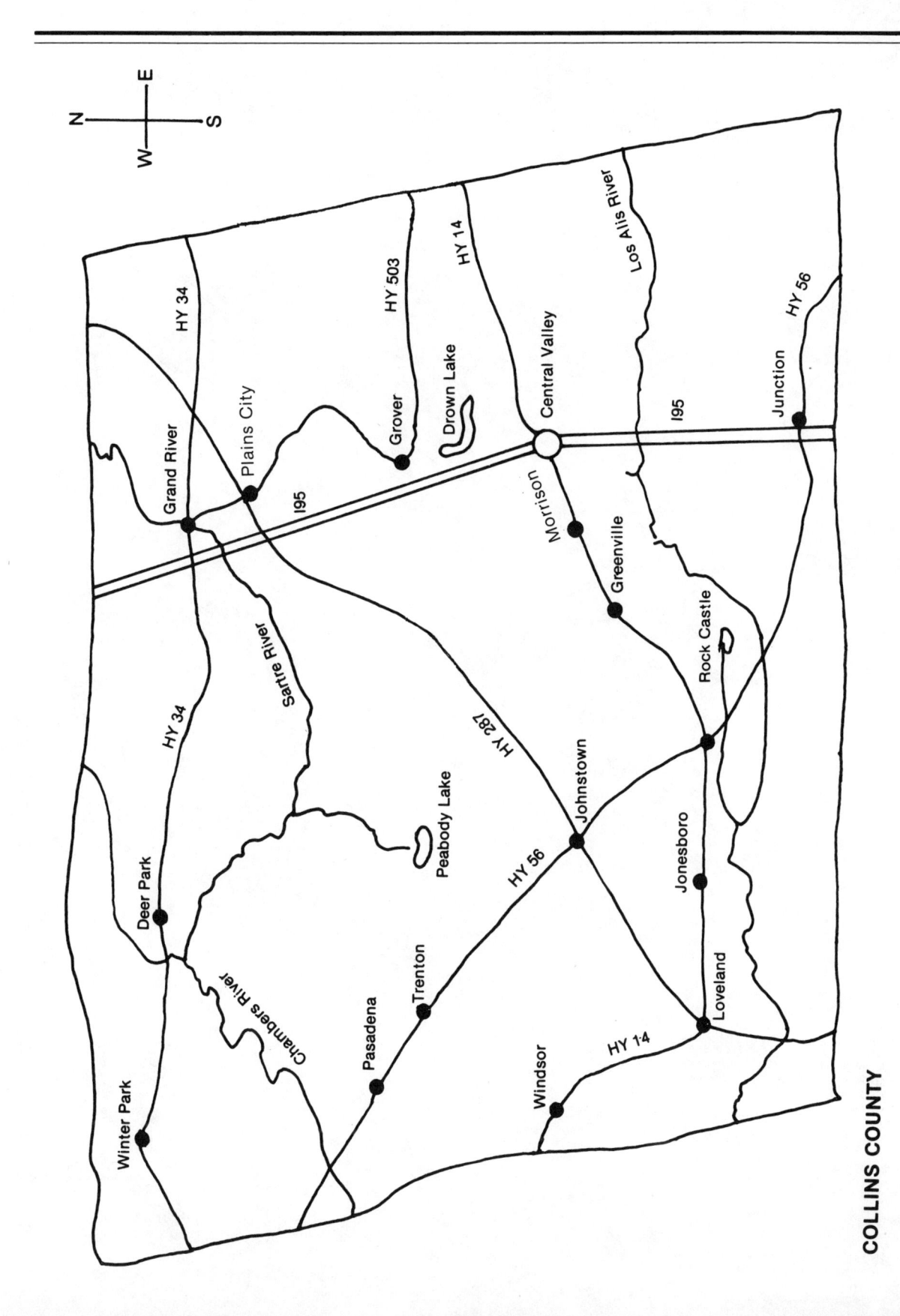

Appendix D

City Directory

Name	Address	Occupation
-A-		
AAA-American Automobile Association	222 Oak	
Alken, Henryken	2521 N. Evans	Outdoor Rec.
Ailes, Stephen	2100 Elizabeth	Businessman
Ajax Cleaners	111 Sylvan Ct.	
Albert, Fred	119 Jones Dr.	Bricklayer
Alexander, Constance L. (Max)	3201 Sycamore	Architect
Alexander, Connie	2120 Kennedy	Student
Alexander, John C. (Millie)	2120 Kennedy	Student
Alexander, Sandra	2127 Georgia	Librarian
Alire, John	621 Sycamore	Policeman
Allen, Terry	143 Briarwood	Student
Alvarez, Abigail C.	16 Norway Dr.	Secretary
Alvarez, Karen	520 E. Laural	Teacher
Ames, John	775 W. Lake	Baker
Amey, Paul	2213 Olive Ct.	Realtor
Anderson, Bean T. (Sherri)	127 Bloomington	Construction laborer
Anderson, Harry	519 N. Loomis	Factory
Anton, John	400 Franklin	Newspaper Reporter
Arkins, Max	528 Pitkin	Trucker
Associated Builders and Contractors	6760 W. Laurel	Union
Atkins, Jesse C. (Cathy)	2112½ Oak	Student
Austin, Jesse	744 Daisy	Laborer
Avery, Carl C.	362 Goshen Ave.	Bus driver
Azcock, Charles	1700 LaPorte	Car dealer
-B-		
Backe, Theodore P. (Mary)	1611 Cherry	Professor
Bagby, Victor	1710 Remington	Artist
Bainer, Sherri	215 Parker	Teacher
Barnes, Marvin	511 Westfall	Student
Bauer, Randy	215 S. Loomis	Policeman
Baum, John	2122 Plum	Policeman
Baxter, Wayne	287 LaPorte	Salesman
Becker, Judson M. (Sue)	764 Alpine	Engineer
Beeks, Bruce	605 S. College	Restaurant
Begonia, Bessie (Alfred)	19 Flower Dr.	Homemaker
Behnke, Larry	142 Hillcrest	Technician
Belew, Dennis	601 So. Howes	Student
Benbow, Bert L.	4521 Edwards	Mgr.-Lumber Co.

Bender, Milo (Lois)	3699 Cape Cod Dr.	Professor
Bewley, Clarence	2712 N. Ellis	Politician
Bloom, Dave	1305 Luke	Singer
Blaker, Frank	1616 Buckeye	Executive
Bob's Bake Shop	1812 S. College	
Boss, Robert K.	108 Black	Unemployed
Brennan, Peter J.	677½ Newsom	Retired
Brewster, Silvia Z.	261 Cat Eye Dr.	Realtor
Britton, Ben L. (Brenda)	1020 Patton	Factory worker
Brown, Jeff	617 Aggie Rd.	Student
Bullwinkle, Bruce M. (Ann)	806 Rocky Rd.	Lawyer
Burke, Rev. Mark M. (Susan)	303 Indiana Place	Minister

-C-

Callaway, Earl	1026 Sycamore	Insurance
Calvin, Mack	21 S. University	Prof. Athlete
Capri, Paul	511 S. Meldrum	Public relations
Carson, Joe	412 Hawkins	Pilot
Castalano, Stan T. (Maggie)	418 Hit	Import/Export
Caster, Julian J. (Laurie)	810 Catcher Rd.	Student
Caswell, Anna	1305 Lemay	Housewife
Catlin, James R. (Alice)	516 Fort Ave.	Ski shop owner
Central Valley Free Press	2120 Stuart	
Central Valley Lumber Co.	Hwy 287	
Central Valley National Bank	2250 University	
Central Valley University	1750 S. Platte River Dr.	
Chitty, Judy	1705 Matthews	Secretary
Cleveland, Reggie	712 Magnolia	Baseball pitcher
Click, Bill	112 Colorado	Professor
Cloal, Virgil	217 Remington	Undertaker
Cohan, Steve	411 S. Mason	Auto mechanic
Cole, Orson	317 Edwards	Actor
Cole, Russell (Vivian)	805 Stan Ave.	Sales
Collins, J. T.	2530 Elm	Janitor
Conway, Timothy (Tim)	3670 Maple	Governor
Cornell, James	1101 Elm	Accountant
Cortesi, Sam (Rebecca)	1778 Trinidad	Factory worker
Costello, Mike R. (Mary)	224 Oxford Dr.	Restaurant owner
Country Cooking Restaurant	411 W. Mountain	
Crupton, Shaun S.	1821 Lipton	Elementary teacher
Cups, Arthur T. (Sharon)	327 Saucer Rd.	Telephone repairman
Cutter, Rev. Stephen L. (Sal)	835 Sanford	Minister

-D-

Daigle, Bill	1780 Terry Lake	Computer technician
Davis, Bruce	1521 N. Temple	Pilot
Dale, Chris	614 Overland Trail	Student
Damon, Herb	1412 N. Shields	Fireman
Dan's Deli	412 W. Prospect	
Dary, James W. (Cicley)	214 S. Bend Ave.	Factory worker
Dash, Don	307 S. Sherwood	Auctioneer
Davis, Susan	4 Alcott	Student
Day, Peter	505 Wood	Physicist
Dennis, Dick	233 McKinley	Policeman
Dinkel, Earl	801 E. Drake	Laborer

Name	Address	Occupation
Diwitt, Robert	744 Oxford	Merchant
Dixon, Richard	211 E. Oak	Electrical engineer
Douglas, W. G. (Moira)	932 Ash Lane	Factory vice-president
Doyle, Carl	571 Drake Apt. 3	Student
Doyle, William Newport	2550 S. Prospect	Student
Driscoll, Mary	577 Webster	Lawyer

-E-

Eastland, James	1212 Trinidad	Lawyer
Ebel, Lyle	2000 W. Plum	Florist
Edwin, W. Richard (Edna)	243 Maiden Lane	X-Ray technician
Eggers, Kathy	231 McKinly	Housewife
Eisler, Edward C.	624 W. California	Gas station attendant
Elbel, Lybel	11235 N. Aimes	Florist
Elder, Lee	317 Remington	Golfer
Electrical Surplus	612 Linden	
Elks Club	14 E. Oak	
Ellgood, Omar	1504 Teakwood	Repairman
Ellis, Tom	310 Sherwood	Newscaster
Elmore, Norm	819 Matthews	Cameraman
English, Sam J. (Andrea)	1772 S. Roosevelt	Factory foreman
Ethan, Paul (Sally)	202 W. Olly	Motel manager
Euke, Joe	504 Alpert	Policeman
Evans, Pat	1812 Crestmore	Cook
Everitt, Steve	200 Jefferson	Dog catcher
Eyers, Don	632 Stover	Janitor

-F-

Fain, Linda	105 Columbia	Engineer
Farley, Larry	1607 Larch	Factory worker
Faron, Steven	600 E. Plum	Retired
Feit, Norm	254 W. Prospect	City Manager
First Baptist Church	1102 Kirkwood	
First Lutheran Church	500 Webster	
First Presbyterian Church	249 E. Main	
First United Methodist	243 W. Grove	
Flinn, Ed	507 N. Grant	Lawyer
Foreman, Rob	900 Webster	Bus driver
Fort Collins Calendar Co.	1190 Mountain	
Fort Collins Catholic Church	500 Fort Ave.	
Foster, Eugene J. (Sheryl)	81 Western Pl.	Clothing store owner
Foster, Fred T. (Sharon)	88 Western Pl.	Engineer
Foster, James	2522 S. 5th Ave.	Policeman
Fountain, Sam	3561 Hanover	Retired
Fowler, Bobby	330 Alpert	Student
Fowler, James (Denise)	324 Alpert	Student
Franks, Barry	400 Hickory	Hotel owner
Fritz, Lance	19 Onieada	Laundromat owner
Froome, William	8170 Gable	Businessman
Fulton, Matt	2709 Harvard	Painter
Fuqua, George	1101 Smith	Bar owner

-G-

Gauce, Samuel L.	2501 Jamie	Mgr. of Bus System
Gabel, Dan	536 Sheldon	Factory worker

Name	Address	Occupation
Gagnon, Larry	1000 Lemay	Electrician
Galleger, Rory	420 S. Loomis	Cement Plant Mgr.
Garrett, Mike	530 LaPorte	Auto mechanic
Garrity, Pat	1232 S. Bryan	Police Chief (acting)
Gerber, Mark	312 Poudre	Student
Ghent Mobile Homes	1005 E. Elizabeth	
Gilmore, Artis	503 Matthews	Barber
Gimble, Hank	710 Eastdale	Jeweler
Glass, Chip	213 Thunderbird	Pro football player
Glover, Gary	215 Del Clair	Construction worker
Glutz, Elmer C. (Emily)	616 Court	Insurance salesman
Good, Samuel B. (Betsy)	32 Berry Blvd.	Construction worker
Grace, Edward	75 N. Scarlett	Lawyer
Great Rocky Mountain Lumber Co.	Hwy 12	
Green, James J. (Kathy)	522 Grant	Psychologist
Groulx, Leon	2122 W. Timnath	Motel manager
Gurney, Sam G.	1520 W. Roosevelt	Policeman

-H-

Name	Address	Occupation
Haisty, Don	1104 Sycamore	Student
Hale, Mary Ann	646 Apple Lane	Lumber Co. mgr.
Halls, H. A.	5120 Raleigh	Politician
Halpin, Ed	1305 Kirkwood	Ski salesman
Hammer, Mark J.	212½ Trinidad	Student
Hansen, Joe	1117 City Park Ave.	Unemployed
Hancock, John J. (Beverly)	16 Stubbs	Assistant to Mayor
Hardin, Kevin	340 Mohegan	Construction
Hardman, Cedric	241 Dale Ct.	Lawyer
Hardy, Harriet R.	10 Libber Lane	Factory foreman
Harner, Ed (Francis)	556 Lake	Advertising
Harris, Kenneth Jr.	2570 Zenith	Reporter
Harris, R. C.	2371 Sony	Civil service
Harris, Ronald, Dr.	617 Peterson	Doctor
Hart, Van	2102 Custom	State senator
Hasty, Don	1104 Sycamore	Businessman
Haswell, Anthony	3359 W. Kramer	Railroad president
Hayes, Susan (Leonard)	1818 Paster Ave.	Nurse
Henry, James	219 W. Roosevelt	Gas station owner
Hersloff, John	928 James Ct.	Waiter
Heston, Charleton	3371 Court	Actor
Hezlep, Joyce	173 Hillcrest	Social worker
Hicks, Lloyd	3001 E. Locust	Football Coach
Hilton, Brian	17 Choppin	Police Captain
Hines, Sally	1530 Ruby	Student
Holiday Music Co.	2164 S. College	
Holland, Carolyn O.	756 S. Bend Ave.	Boutique owner
Holmes, John (Becky)	364 Webster	Police captain
Holt, Thomas	2150 Orange	Golf course director
Hooper, Jon K. (Grace)	725 Allison Ave.	Sewage chemist
Hot, Rock	1943 S. Main	Bar owner
Hughes, Clarence G. (Dorothy)	613 N. Bend Ave.	Judge
Human Society for Collins County	216 College	
Hydrox, Helen (Ralph)	514 Nabisco	Homemaker

-J-

Name	Address	Occupation
Jackson, David L. (Melody)	425 Princeton Rd.	Retired machinist

Jackson, George (Diane)	1987 Patton Ave.	Marine general, retired
Jackson, Henry	1660 Tejon	Zoo keeper
Jacobs, Katherine L.	129 Sherry Place	Owner of Doll Hospital
Jakobi, William	516 S. Meldrum	Accountant
Jarvis, Ray	2613 Sanford	Farmer
Jason, Michael	718 Beech	Novelist
Jeabson, Glenn	2824 E. Harmony	Owner of Poor Boys
Jenkins, Jerry J. Jr.	5521 N. Ellis	Businessman
Jenkins, Jerry J. (Rose)	6212 Summit Ridge Dr.	Owner of Campus Shop
Jenkins, Jerry Jr.	1716 S. Oak	Mgr. of Campus Shop
Jennings, Peter	2516 Terry Lake Rd.	Janitor
Jirak, Charles	1221 S. Bryan	Electrical technician
Joder, Thomas	407 Wood	Track coach
Johns, Harold (Betty)	91 Coursey Blvd.	Pastor
Johnson, Chester	2160 Skull Rd.	Retired
Johnson, George	2150 Filmore	Politician
Johnson, James P.	109 N. Apricot	Professor
Johnson, Kim	2130 W. Hill Dr.	Congressman
Johnson, Karl	2420 Crabtree Dr.	Liquor store owner
Jones Auto Sales	1014 N. College	
Jones, Gordon J.	371 Ash Lane	Stockbroker
Jones, Elwood	659 LaJunta	Clerk
Jones, John	7211 Ashley Dr.	Lawyer
Jones, Robert L.	1101 Crab	Trash collector
Jones, Suzy	2130 Proverb	Secretary
Joy, Pam	4509 S. Country Rd. 13	Dental Assistant
Jung, Karl	509 E. Lake	Psychologist

-K-

Karr, Roger	1124 Parkwood	Musician
Kask, Oscar, Dr.	634 Matthews	Dentist
Keil, Rudy	718 Winchester	Ad business
Kelly, William	3520 S. Loomis	Agronomist
Kelsey, Sam (Sue)	2532 Lincoln St.	Air Force
Kerr, Ewing T.	1112 E. Matthews	Judge
Kelso, Willard	412 W. Laurel	Horse breeder
Kendall, Penny	508 Westwood	Real estate
Ken's Ski Shop	2418 W. Mountain	
Kemp, Jack	108 Princeton	Insurance
Kershner, Don	120 W. Lake	Promoter
Kesson, Albert	2081 S. Taft Hill	Tree surgeon
Kidd, William	1906 Pecan	Ski instructor
Kimball, Carl Ray	815½ Lake	Manager of Walden's
Kimbell, Jeff A.	355 Galaxy	Clerk
Kincaid, Jeb	2520 E. Mulberry	T.V. producer
Kiwanis Club	111 N. College	
Knocks, Beverly	2122 Ingersoll	Food service worker
Knowles, George	8590 Simpson	Photographer

-L-

Lake, John	1300 Teakwood	Architect
Lakeside Landscape	618 Terry Lake Rd.	
Lamb, Lamle (Susan)	16-C Aggie Village	Student
Lantnz, George (Pam)	312 Wayne	Factory worker
Larco, J. B.	2112 Shields	CVU president

Name	Address	Occupation
Larzun, Gary (Lois)	1305 Burton Ct.	Lawyer
LaRue, Buddy	505 E. Prospect	Landscaper
LaRue, Lillian P.	2 Spice Rd.	Cashier
Latimer, Tom C. (Susan)	221 E. Elm	Student
Lawrence, John C. (Terri)	521 Lance Circle	Professor
Leach, Bert (Linda)	1316 W. Oak	Trucker
Lee, Samuel (Betty)	483 Franklin	Doctor
Lennon, John	409 Columbia	Hairdresser
Levy, Job J. (Cynthia)	906 Palm Ave.	Deli owner
Lewis, Harry	2580 N. National	Zoologist
Link, Steve (Mary)	228 W. Prospect	Furniture sales
Linoel, James (Leslie)	668 Twin Dr.	Carpenter
Lions Club	2122 N. Round	
Little, Constance F.	954 Lipton	Student
Locust, Ted	6150 E. Zombie	Politician
Lopez, Matt (Teresa)	726 Sherry	Unemployed
Lopez, Terry (Irene)	728 Sherry	Salesman
Louden, Tim (Barbara)	324 Eli	Pipefitter
Lucas, Andrew, Dr.	101 Blue	Physician
Lucas, Simon N., Dr. (Val)	318 W. Smith	Doctor
Lylte, Lillian	108 Black	Secretary

-M-

Mabez, Joan	414 Church	Secretary
Mack, Bob (Maria)	2960 Dean	Shoe repairman
Madicon, Earl (Effie)	308 E. Oak	Owner of hardware store
Madison, James	7521 Green	Retired
Maier, Patrick (Pat)	1445 Edora	Plumber
Manuel, Ben (Robbie)	120 N. Lyons	Banker
Marks, Dee	2171 N. Boston	Information officer
Martin, Frank	2530 Smith Rd.	City Safety director
Marrs, Gene	1638 E. Mulberry	Salesman
Marshall, James R. (Ruth)	351 Lakewood	City planner
Mason, T. E. (Sylvia)	171 Grove Terrace	Taxi driver
Mathis, Floyd (Gertrude)	27 Woodland Ave.	Prize fighter
Matzner, William (Nona)	416 LaPorte	Student
Maybon, Hank	221 Matthews	Cook
McDonald, Marlene	5511 N. Custom Dr.	Health Lab supervisor
McIver, Fred	172 Hillcrest	Real estate
McGee, Daniel C.	5512 Settler Ave.	Real Estate
McGee, Robert J.	5512 Settler Ave.	Real Estate
McLain, Joseph R.	1880 Clean Ave.	Street supt.
McNutt, Grady (Sheryl)	2837 Sumac	Policeman
Metropolitan Episcopal Church	125 N. 3rd	
Miles, Bill	7552 Loretta	Sales at Central Dry
Miller, John (Marlene)	16 Chalet Ct.	Coach
Milles, William S.	3121 No Gates	Professor
Mitchell, Paul S. (Rhonda)	112 E. 5th Ave.	High School coach
Moore, Sally	1667 N. Schaeffer	Secretary
Morris, Peter (Pat)	411 S. Court	T.V. repairman
Moses, Carlos S.	2055 Sunshine	Politician
Mosner, Joseph R.	161 James Ave.	CVU Lacrosse coach
Mover, Maxine C.	185 Lovelace Ave.	SDD housemother
Munson, Robert	2021 Moore Pl.	Lawyer
Murphey, Leonard (Barbara)	6671 Head Road	Owner of ski shop

Name	Address	Occupation
Murray, Roger W.	2530 W. Sanity	Banker

-N-

Name	Address	Occupation
Nagel, Calvin	7920 SE Frontage	Developer
Nanta, Howard (Lois)	1933 Yorktown	Optometrist
Napoleon, Tim	201 E. Bing	Librarian
Nayman, John	3140 South St.	Student
Never, Charles (Eva)	3001 Mallard	Judge
Nevis, Henry E.	1943 S. Main	Owner of bar
Nezer, Paul R. (Sally)	1132 Lakewood	Teacher
Nichols, Barry (Laura)	605 Plum	Sales
Nix, Gordon (Mabel)	421 S. Howes	Mayor
Norris, Chris	905 N. College	City councilman
Northern Colorado Electric	1799 S. College	
Norton, Perry (Alice)	1648 Larch	Motorcycle repair
Noyes, Peggy (Fred)	220 E. Laurel	Garage owner
Nunn, Anne	230 Cherry	Nurse
Nystrom, Al (Grace)	206 W. Mountain	Roofer

-O-

Name	Address	Occupation
Oates, Phil (Nonette)	1220 Southbridge	Policeman
O'Brien, Bruce W.	6170 S. Colorado Dr.	Asst. professor
O'Brien, Jim (Carolyn)	420 Impala	Stockbroker
O'Cooney, Timothy I.	1984 Coors Place	Tavern owner
Odom, Thomas	1321 Luke	Florist
O'Donnell, Cletus	2530 N. Main	Bishop
Olson, Phil Q. (Ingrid)	3112 Locust	Upholster repair
Orcutt, Steve P. (Pam)	308 Gordon	Tire salesman
Oreo, Jason L. (Paula)	2115 S. Howes	Asst. pastor
Osuch, Peter (Dorothy)	809 Tyler	Bus driver
Overton, Ernest W. (Dawn)	816 W. Myrtle	Theatre owner
Owen, Ralph	371 Sherwood	Unemployed
Ozark Optical	529 W. Mountain	

-P-

Name	Address	Occupation
Paben, Tony (Martha)	127 Grant	CVU wrestling coach
Paget, Sloan (Elizabeth)	710 Colorado	Welder
Pallansch, Sigrrid (Jane)	8114 Maynard	Exterminator
Palos, Frank	233 N. Meldrum	Picture framer
Parker, Helen	25 N. Spalding	Parks recreation super.
Parr, James (Betsy)	33 Country Club Road	Post office
Paul, Clara	2991 Oneida	Finance analyst
Peabody, Joyce T.	1112 Rocky Road	Advertising artist
Penn Paint Company	3326 LaPorte Ave.	
Perkins, Jay	4042 Oak	Reporter
Perkins, Kelly	121 Florida	Rodeo clown
Peters, William	20 College Ave.	Student
Pine, Rutherford L. (Dell)	101 Alien Drive	Retired
Pinon, Dirk J. (Susan)	2721 Ellis, Grover	Retired
Pinon, Larry P. (Maria)	6412 Ash Lane	Maintenance
Powers, Jay (Nellie)	517 Main	Construction
Preston, Louise	510 Peterson	Retired

-Q-

Name	Address	Occupation
Quaid, Irvin R. (Eva)	1551 Briarwood	Undertaker

Query, Randall T. (Adria)	906 Matthews	Drywaller
Quigley, Frank (Velma)	2401 Lake	Coroner
Quinn, Ed. (Diana)	111 Hillcrest	CPA
Quinta, Larry	126 Sylvan	Gasomat attendant

-R-
Rager, John	1949 Arlington	Student
Rainey, Sid (Arlene)	2118 Ridelawn	Painter
Ramada Inn	6110 S. College	
Randall, Harry	120 Kennedy	Movie Director
Ratcliff, Duane	1304 Lawrence Dr.	Hairdresser
Redfield, Carl (Agnes)	1919 Wequassett Rd.	Salesman
Republican Party	601 Shields	
Retreat, Louis	1671 Nugget Rd.	Professor
Reynolds Funeral Home	6742 Frankenstein	
Rhead, Ronald (Hilda)	3128 Wayne	Retired
Rich, David	2330 N. Matthews	TV Newscaster
Richter, James	8112 Conoco Way	Fireman
Richter, Jerry (Mary)	1218 S. Bryant	Policeman
Richter, Ned	8121 S. Jones	Retired
Reidy, Carol	1451 Horseshoe Dr.	Social worker
Roadflower, Roberta C.	248 Blossom Ave.	Horticulturist
Roam, Randall J. (Julie)	5514 Settler	News reporter
Roat, John J.	456 Main	Artist
Rogers, Walter	359 Job	Union leader
Rolf, Paul	12 Morrison Dr.	Morrison Mayor
Roser, Robert R.	4849 Sheboygan Ave.	Busboy
Ross, Dwight	1955 Hoover	Musician
Ruth, Robert J. (Bonnie)	161 Ashland	District attorney

-S-
Sadler, Dick	105 Stuart	Railroad public relations
Sagert, Norman (Arlene)	1313 Robertson	Apt. manager
Sanchez, Leo R.	1800 W. 44th Ave.	Painter
Sanders, Cheryl	542 Webster	Student
Sanders, Ken L. (Mary)	542 Webster	School superintendent
Sandoval, Fred	2530 Leisure Dr.	Sheet metal worker
Sauer, Fred P. (Georgia)	101 Silent Hills	Plumber
Saxon, John R. (Brenda)	331 E. Magnolia	Junk yard owner
Schlonck, Willy (Willa)	3232 Lincoln Rd.	Retired
Seaman, Carl Wayne	2550 N. Lowrey	Dry cleaner owner
Second National Bank	112 Hested	
Segrest, Paul (Nancy)	400 Duke Lane	Tavern owner
Shaw, Rick	115 Rutgers	Brick mason
Shell Oil Refinery	Deer Park; Hwy 287	
Siciliano, Tony	125 Temple	Student
Sigma Delta Delta	CVU Campus	
Simon, Gerald E.	2995 Kennedy Blvd.	Developer
Skiller, James J. (Ruth)	999 Elephant	City councilman
Skitt, Daniel L. (Patsy)	8233 Harvard	Truck driver
Smith, Dwight	163 Bright	Democratic Chairman
Smith, George	2651 Myrtle	Pastor
Smith, Louis	15 E. Arizona	Salesman
Smith, Paul	21 S. Newsom	Welder
Smith, Sam G.	2331 N. Water	Medical doctor

Name	Address	Occupation
Smith, Tom J.	2070 S. Mench	Professor
Smitherman, Elliot	111 N. St. Paul	Politician
Smitherman, John C. (Ellie)	6064 W. 77th	Judge
Smitherman, John S.	318 W. Smith Ave.	Retired
Smythe, Charles P. (Karen)	111 Elite Circle	Retired
Snelling, Rev. J. J. (Hilda)	2561 Manze Ave.	Minister
Spencer, Tom	511 N. Loomis	Carpenter
Steppes, John	2581 Whitcombe	Pastor
Sunshine Laundromat	2922 Elizabeth	
Swish, Tim	127 Pearl	Businessman
Snyder, Tom (Kathy)	34 B Aggie Village	Student
Snyder, W. Kevin (Kathy)	614 Aggie Village	Student

-T-

Name	Address	Occupation
Tagge, Jerry (Paula)	423 Franklin	Pilot
Takenda, Larry	705 Sunrise	Real estate salesman
Tandem, Abigail M. (Randy)	555 Yale	Retired
Tappen, Matt	116 Franklin	Auto mechanic
Taylor, Earl	2230 Firewood	Retired
Taylor, Ted (Janie)	Hwy 287	Owner of Ted's Place
Temble, Bob Dr. (Sarah)	1987 Boglue	Doctor
Thompson, Steven	4132 Huntington	Professor
Thompson, Herman	HWY 14	Ranch owner
Trimmer, John P.	7560 Quincy	Union president

-U-

Name	Address	Occupation
Uarco, Lynn (Ruth)	19C Aggie Village	Student
Udick, Bob (Paula)	503 Hanna	Forest ranger
Underhill, Ed (Betty)	Paudre Canyon	Veterinarian supplier
Unger, Frank Dr. (Sandra)	210 W. Magnider	Doctor
United, Howard	617 Marston Ln.	Parks & recreation dir.
United Supply	679 S. Howes	
Unser, Bob	2940 E. 16th	Car mechanic

-V-

Name	Address	Occupation
Vadar, Robert (Mona)	716 Peterson	Teacher
Valdez, Frank (Theresa)	1319 W. Mulberry	Policeman
Valley Country School	1500 E. James	
Van de Meer, Al (Diane)	1026 Larkspur	Painter
Vigil, Herb (Maggie)	808 Oxford	Factory worker
Voss, Ed (Edith)	775 W. Lake	Electrical engineer

-W-

Name	Address	Occupation
Wagg, Al (Ola)	306 W. Whitcomb	FBI
Wagner, Rob	658 Remington	Pizza Hut owner
Waker, Jerry	2122 N. Simms	Student
Waldren, Chuck (Margaret)	2099 Berkley	Safeway manager
Walker, Jerry T. (Jenny)	6208 Harvard	Student
Walker, Steve (Zelma)	1188 Westward	Unemployed
Wall, Steve	127 Mason	Post Office
Walsh, Sue	110 W. Howes	Waitress
Wang, Henry	1917 S. Shields	Tailor
Washington Hotel	636 Washington	
Weber, Sam	22 E. Lake	Actor
Weiner, Hugh J. (Mary)	789 Holcomb	Musician

Name	Address	Occupation
Welch, Raquel	2530 Hollywood Dr.	Actress
White, Charles H.	2891 Hall	Politician
Whitmire, Carol	10 Allen Ave.	Sheriff
Whitney, Keith	1255 Job	Pastor
Whitter, Abe R. (Sarah)	990 W. Olive	Teacher
Will, Daniel R. (Marsha)	2122 N. Simms	Bus driver
Wills, Joel (Shirley)	730 Meadows	Teacher
Williams, Chet W.	7011 S. Knoll	Politician
Willis, James J.	123 W. Lake Apt. 10	Student
Wilson, Jack	709 Logan	Writer
Wood, Carol	130 Riverbend	Professor
Woolco Department Store	191 S. College	
Wright, Ross E.	162 W. Mountain	Librarian
Wynn, Roger K.	218 City Circle	Retired

-X-

Name	Address	Occupation
XYZ Motel	1520 Washington	

-Y-

Name	Address	Occupation
Yager, Robert	917 James	Retired
Yancy, Carl (Marty)	788 Colorado	Lawyer
Yazid, Tom (Cynthia)	1980 W. Lake	Judge
York, Michael	2941 Franklin	Student
York, Randall	450 Country Club Rd.	Physician
York, Robert R.	6120 Spruce	Owner of lumber co.
Young, James (Millicent)	698 Tulane	Pilot
Young, Paul (Stacy)	2122 Englewood	Retired
Young, Sam	Box 2104, Hwy 287	Bank president
Youth Products, Inc.	1316 Adams Lane	
Yule, Al	115 W. Laurel	News reporter

-Z-

Name	Address	Occupation
Zem, Richard	921 Meade	Judge
Ziegler, Ronald (Danielle)	1789 Ussez	Personnel Director

***Street names that are not marked, Ave., Road are streets.

***The wife's name is in parenthesis; however, if husband's name is in parenthesis, he is deceased.